Mongolian Church and Missionary Challenges

Rita A. Callicoat

Abstract

This is born from the realisation that the Mongolian cross-cultural missionary movement is at a pivotal stage in its lifecycle. This flourishing movement stems from a first-generation church, a church that emerged only after the country's break from Soviet-style communism and its embracing of multi-party democracy in 1991. Yet there appears to be dysfunctional independence rather than coherence within the cross-cultural missionary movement. Consequently, this dissertation first sought to understand and evaluate the current cross-cultural missionary movement and, from this evaluation and analysis of the why question, to develop a strategy that begins to aid coherence and possibly develop a healthy interdependence within the movement towards growth and sustainability.

Part I explores the biblical and practical elements necessary for an emerging missionary movement from the Majority-World and continues by painting a contextual portrait of the Mongolian church. As the heart of the research, part II uses data from semi-structured interviews conducted across the movement to begin the evaluation. At the same time, focus group participants discussed particular challenges for the movement. Next, gaining insight into the strengths, weaknesses, and challenges of this young movement, this study presents the possible formation of a strategic plan in part III. This plan is designed to strengthen the apparent fragile relationship between the sending churches and the sending agencies, enabling both parties to clarify their role and responsibility while working as a unified missionary movement. Elements within this plan are carefully designed to address particular theological and cultural issues highlighted during the interviews. Finally, this dissertation offers several further studies that would be useful for the Mongolian church to pursue and contemplates how this research could be a valuable case study example for similar research that might be needed in former Soviet-influenced nations in Central Asia.

Table of Contents

Table of Contents vi

List of Tables xi

List of Figures xii

List of Maps xiii

List of Abbreviations xiv

Introduction to and Rationale for this Study 1
    A Brief History of The Mongolian Cross-Cultural Missionary
        Movement 3
    Background 4
    Research Design 5
        Purpose 5
        Goal 5
        Central Research Issue 6
        Research Questions 6
        Application Intent Question 6
        Significance 6
        Key Definitions 7
        Assumptions 8
        Delimitations 9
        Limitations 10
        Dissertation Overview 11
    Summary 12

Part I Exploring Core Elements of a Cross-Cultural Missionary Movement 13

Chapter 1 Fixed in God: The Rightful Place of Church and Mission 14

From Ecclesiocentric Mission to a Theocentric Mission 14
    The Church and Mission Relationship Through the Centuries ... 15
    The Emergence of *Missio Dei* as the Centre of Mission 16
    The Role of the Church in the *Missio Dei* 18
Forming and Sustaining a Movement 20
    Collective Behaviour Theory 21
        Resource Mobilisation Theory (RM) 22
        New Social Movements (NSMs) 22
    Organisational Elements 26
    Organisational Culture 26
    Structure, Goals, and Personnel 28
        Structure 28
        Goals 28
        Personnel 29
    Sustainable Elements 31
        Partnerships 32
        Networks 35
Summary 37

Chapter 2   Majority-World Indigenous Missionary Movements 39
African Missionary Movements 40
    Emerging Missionary Movements 41
    Ghana: The Church of Pentecost (CoP) 43
    Zimbabwe: *Rukwadzano* 45
    Summary 46
Asian Missionary Movements 47
    The Korean Missionary Movement (KMM) 48
        Explosive Growth 48
        God's Perfect Timing 49
        Precautionary Elements of the KMM 49
        Positive Elements 50
    Singaporean Success 51
    Asian Missionary Movements (AMMs) 52
    Summary 53
Latin American Missionary Movements 54
    COMIBAM: 55
    Integral Mission 56
Summary 58

Chapter 3   Good Soil: A Mongolian Contextual Portrait 59
Historical Background 60
Religion and Culture 64
    Religious Persuasions 64
    Cultural Keys 65
Contemporary Political and Economic Status 67

The Mongolian Church: First-Generation Implications 69
    The Journey of Christianity in Mongolia.....................................70
    The Mongolian Cross-Cultural Missionary Movement...............72
Summary..74

Part II Understanding the Here and Now While Looking to the Potential of the Future 76

Chapter 4 Methodology for Gathering the Data 77
    Research Challenges: COVID-19 and Security Issues...............77
    Research Rationale and Choice of Methods 78
        Personal Background 79
        The Issue Being Addressed..80
    The Research Sample..81
        Size of Sample Populations 82
        Representation of Sample Populations 83
    Accessing the Research Population 84
    Protocol for the Research Process..85
    Methods: The Tools Used to Gather the Information.................85
    Data Collection 86
        Semi-Structured Interviews 86
        Focus Groups 89
    Pre Testing 90
    Limitations to Findings..91
    Reliability and Validity..92
    Summary..93

Chapter 5 The Findings:..94

The Current Mongolian Missionary Movement and Paths Forward 94
    The Process of Data Analysis 95
    Using Brant's Categorisation for Initial Analysis of the Data.............96
        Calling..96
        Visionary Leaders 98
            Direction 98
            Leadership..99
        Missional Churches..99
        Appropriate Training 101
        Flexible Structures 103
        Sustainable Finances 104
        Prayer..106
        Summary...107
    Analysis of Key Research Results 108
        Unity, Disunity Dichotomy..108
        Nomadic Lifestyle Influences..111

Children's Education 114
Healthcare 115
Structural Weaknesses and Missiological Grounding 116
Adizes' Lifecycle Analysis 117
Analysis Through Bolman and Deal's Four Frames 120
Theological, Missiological and Socioeconomic Struggles
.... 126
The Korean Influence on the Movement 128
Summary 130

Part III Moving Forward: Growing and Sustaining a Cross-Cultural Missionary Movement 133

Chapter 6 Implications of the Findings and Necessary Changes to Grow and Sustain This Movement 134
Discoveries That Point the Way Forward 135
Implications of the Findings 137
Developing a Strategic Plan for a Stronger Future 140
People Involved in the Proposed Strategic Development Plan. 141
Sending Churches Leadership 142
Sending Agency Leadership 143
Mongolian Cross-Cultural Missionary Movement
Influencers 144
The Mongolian Mission Partnership (MMP) 145
How Might the Participants Respond? 146
A Strategy Towards a Stronger Future 148
Pre-Plan Inaugural Meeting 148
Establishing the Centrality of the Church in Mission ... 149
Acknowledging the Equal Value of Church and Agency
in Mission 149
Recognising, Respecting and Learning to Defer to One
Another 150
Discovering How to Build Up and Encourage One
Another 151
Timeframe 152
Summary 152

Conclusions and Recommendations 154
Conclusion: Growing and Sustaining a Mongolian Cross-Cultural
Missionary Movement 155
Implications Beyond Mongolia 158
Recommendations for Further Studies 159
Concluding Remarks 160

List of Tables

Table 1: Aspects of the Missionaries' Calling 97

Table 2: Sending Church Leaders' Expressions of Missional Church............................100

Table 3: Participants' comments About Appropriate Training 103

Table 4: Participants' Comments on the Need for Unity 110

Table 5: participants' Comments on the Apparent Disunity 111

Table 6: Results of the Two Cultural Values Studies Used for this Analysis 112

List of Figures

Figure 1: The Cultural Onion 27

Figure 2: The Imperatives of Partnership Design 35

Figure 3: Adizes Lifecycle Diagram 118

Figure 4: An Integrated Mongolian Cross-Cultural Missionary Movement 138

Figure 5: Church & Mission Agencies Together 139

Figure 6: Pictorial Summary of the Dissertation Discoveries 157

List of Maps

Map 1: The Former Mongol Empire in Today's World 80

List of Abbreviations

CL	Sending Church Leader
CM	Cross-Cultural Missionary
CoP	Church of Pentecost
DTS	Discipleship Training School
FG	Focus Group
KMM	Korean Missionary Movements
MMP	Mongolian Mission Partnership
NSMs	New Social Movements
RM	Resource Mobilisation
SA	Sending Agency Leader
YWAM	Youth With A Mission

Introduction to and Rationale for this Study

How would we fare if asked to sketch a map of the world from memory? Like many high school students attempting the same task, our maps may display disproportionate continent sizes and have various island groups missing. Yet, it would probably include a dominant swath of colour[1] representing the modern-day Russian Federation and underneath, China. Doubtless, in many of these maps, sandwiched in between like a deflated rugby ball, would appear Mongolia. However, thirty years ago this same exercise might have produced not too dissimilar maps except for one significant difference; the majority would probably be missing Mongolia. Consequently, something happened during the last thirty years to put Mongolia on the map.

In 1921 Russia aided Mongolia to gain independence from China's grip. From this point, Mongolia began fading into the mists of time and the legends of Genghis Khan, disappearing from the political map of the Western world as it became subsumed into what was to become the USSR[2] (Rossabi 2005, 31–37; Bilskie and Arnold 2002, 206). However, towards the end of the 1980s, as the former Soviet Union began crumbling Mongolia sought and gained true independence, finally emerging from the shadows of its giant and powerful neighbours. Broken and bankrupt at the time, Mongolia started the slow process of rebuilding its once great nation (2002, 211–12).

---

[1] Since the author of this dissertation is a British citizen, British, Oxford English spellings have been used throughout the document except in cases where quotations, where the author is being cited and where the author has used American English spelling.

[2] The Union of Soviet Socialist Republics (USSR) was officially formed in 1922. Although Mongolia was never an official part of the USSR "it vicariasly asserted complete control over the political, economic and social life of the country" (Bilskie and Arnold 2002, 206).

Traditionally, two dominant religions have influenced Mongolia. Historically, Shamanism has shaped the Mongol peoples; it is the underlying bedrock of their worldview. But since the thirteenth century, upon that bedrock, Buddhism rose as the dominant religion. Adopting Tibetan Buddhism, Mongolia proceeded to morph both Shamanism and Tibetan Buddhism into one, creating Mongolian Buddhism. This merging of these two religions has been described aptly as "local gods appearing in Buddhist dress" (Tsering 1993, 96). For roughly six hundred years this was the religious foundation of the Mongolian people. Despite Nestorian Christians gaining a presence at administrative levels in the former Mongol Empire, Christianity's influence on the people of Mongolia was minimal. Consequently, by the beginning of the twentieth century nearly half the male population were enrolled as lamas, "influencing not just religion but also culture, economy, society, and politics" (Atwood 2009, 325).

During the seventy years of Soviet friendship and surreptitious control, the backbone of Mongolian Buddhist power and authority was slowly eroded, eventually creating a spiritual vacuum. Consequently, in 1990 when Mongolia opened its doors to the rest of the world along with many aid organisations, Western and South Korean Christian missionaries flooded in and Christianity began filling the spiritual vacuum (Rossabi 2005, 40). By the end of the following year the first Mongolian churches had been established, and between 1992 and approximately 2005 the church in Mongolia grew exponentially (Mongolian Evangelical Alliance 2020, 12). As with the records of the early church in the book of Acts, the Holy Spirit was powerfully present demonstrating God's authority and establishing God's church through miracles and healings. Today, there are approximately 46,000 attendees (around 33,000 believers) in the Mongolian church (Mongolian Evangelical Alliance 2020, 18).

Void of any previous indigenous church tradition these emerging congregations naturally formed around the patterns of expatriate missionaries ministering among them.

Church traditions began forming without any conscious recognition; unfortunately, they were neither indigenous nor uniquely Mongolian. The result is that today the church in Mongolia has a distinctly Western or Korean character,[3] and Christianity struggles to find an authentic Mongolian identity despite the desires of the early believers (Becker 1993, 67).

A Brief History of The Mongolian Cross-Cultural Missionary Movement

According to eyewitness accounts,[4] the Mongolian church has been passionate about evangelising from the outset. Towards the end of the Mongolian church's first decade it was clear God was calling some of these young, passionate believers to take the gospel message beyond Mongolia's current borders, deep into the heart of the Mongol diaspora scattered across the lands of the once infamous Mongol Empire. In the first decade of the twenty-first century, the first cross-cultural missionaries were already being sent out onto the mission field (CM3; CM9&10; SA5).

The challenge facing the Mongolian church is how to facilitate a cross-cultural missionary movement that is genuinely Mongolian and sustainable, a truly indigenous movement. As with the established patterns of the Mongolian church, the cross-cultural missionary movement originating from that church has a distinctly Western/South Korean shape forming. Observation suggests that these structures appear to weigh the Mongolian church down with the unnecessary bureaucratic and financial constraints of

---

[3] With the proximity of South Korea to Mongolian and with languages of similar grammatical structure, Korean missionaries have had a significant influence on the growth of the church and constituted a significant proportion of the expatriate missionary community through the past thirty years.

[4] I have deliberately chosen to use the term "eye witness" as these are the accounts of actual Mongolian believers and foreign missionaries who lived through this amazing era. Many have been colleuges and acquaintances during our nearly thirty years in Mongolia. It is form these accounts that historians will one day draw. Some of these accounts constituted part of my MA dissertation through Trinity St. David, in Wales UK. (2012).

their foreign models of mission, creating a dependency upon foreign money and support. Long term, this appears as though it may be unsustainable.

This remarkable story of the past thirty years has led to the questions asked in this dissertation concerning the growing and sustaining of this cross-cultural missionary movement. Therefore, in this dissertation I intend first to evaluate the current cross-cultural missionary movement. Second, I explore the essential elements necessary to building a healthy missionary movement. Finally, I discuss how this Mongolian cross-cultural missionary movement might become more indigenous and sustainable in light of the findings. Before beginning this process, it is necessary to offer a brief background on my credibility to undertake this research project.

Background

I have had the privilege of living and working among the Mongolian people since the spring of 1993. In the early years I was involved with a vocational Bible school, drawing many young people from across the country to Ulaanbaatar, the capital, for a couple of weeks' training every few months. Today many of these young men and women have become significant leaders of churches or are involved in the plethora of Christian organisations established during the last thirty years. Between 1996-2011, my wife and I lived in a rural province capital working alongside a fledgling church. As an extension of that ministry, together with another English couple we established a business (New Beginning Centre Ltd, trading under the name Fairfield), creating employment and discipling opportunities for young Christians in an economically struggling town.[5] In 2014, after three years away from Mongolia, we returned to Ulaanbaatar to serve alongside those called to cross-cultural missionary service among the Mongol diaspora.

---

[5] Fairfield is a café, bakery, and guesthouse emplying around twenty to thirty Monoglian workers throughout the year, prior to COVID-19. However, due to a ban on tourism, this figure has been significantly affected. www.fairfield.mn

I have witnessed the transformation of many of those early young believers into seasoned leaders and significant influencers within the church in Mongolia. Some of those involved in the growing cross-cultural missionary movement acknowledge the struggles the movement faces and recognise the need for good structure and stability. In discussion with these men and women my dilemma is what counsel to offer when approached. This personal quandary, perceived through the lens of the concerns above, formed the basis of this research project. Finally, as an outsider not seeking to lead but rather to inspire and influence the influencers, my role is one of a catalyst. A catalyst, as Brafman and Beckstrom state, "Isn't usually in it for praise and accolades. When his or her job is done, a catalyst knows it's time to move on" (2007, 93). This statement aptly describes my heart's desire and current role in writing this dissertation.

Research Design

This section summarises the framework and key dimensions of this research project. Each of the statements and research questions comprises key components of this dissertation.

Purpose

The purpose of this study is to evaluate the current Mongolian cross-cultural missionary movement and its progress and challenges towards becoming a sustainable indigenous movement now and in the future.

Goal

The goal of this study is to draw conclusions based on my findings that can influence the discussion and promote relevant action towards the development of an indigenous group of people who together will facilitate a sustainable Mongolian cross-cultural missionary movement.

Central Research Issue

The central research issue of this study is to discover key elements integral to developing a sustainable cross-cultural missionary movement within the wider Mongolian Christian context.

Research Questions

1. What are foundational elements necessary to establish a cross-cultural missionary movement?

2. What do select mission pastors recognise as the church's role within the Mongolian cross-cultural missionary movement?

3. What do select Mongolian cross-cultural missionaries recognise as key elements of a sustainable missionary movement?

4. How are select sending agencies supporting and encouraging the Mongolian cross-cultural missionary movement?

Application Intent Question

How might the Mongolian church develop an effective, cohesive, and sustainable cross-cultural missionary movement?

Significance

As a long-term missionary with Pioneers[6] in Mongolia, I expect this research project to be significant personally in better comprehending the complexities of an emerging Majority-World cross-cultural missionary movement. Furthermore, I expect the

---

[6] Pioneers is an international non-denominational mission agency currently working in 104 countries worldwide. www.pioneers.org

study to provide a springboard for the Mongolian church to discuss and implement some of this study's findings and thus develop sustainable structures with reachable targets for the movement's growth. In addition, this study is significant for the collective world of traditional mission movements, often coming from Western nations, in grasping how they might learn to integrate and partner with similar movements emanating from the Majority-World. Finally, acknowledging that the face of mission worldwide is changing (Pocock, Van Rheenen, and McConnell 2005), this research project will provide another piece in the puzzle to understanding a more globally integrated missiology for the worldwide church in the twenty-first century.

Key Definitions

1. Majority-World: This dissertation prefers to use the term Majority-World rather than Global South or Third World to describe Mongolia's political and economic status. Geographically Mongolia struggles to fit into what is considered the Global South (literally) and lies North of what is known as the 10/40 window. Therefore, the term Majority-World is more acceptable, and as missiologist Enoch Wan observes, "it does not carry any negative connotation or judgmental evaluation" (2009, 127).

2. Mongolian and Mongol: According to Encyclopaedia Britannica, Mongol refers to a member of a Central Asian ethnographic people *(The Editors of Encyclopedia Britannica 2020)*, whereas Mongolian refers to someone living in modern-day Mongolia today. Therefore, this dissertation will refer to (i) the Mongolian church and the Mongolian cross-cultural missionary movement, (ii) its former Empire as

the Mongol Empire, and the scattered related people groups as the Mongol diaspora.

Assumptions

I assume in this dissertation that it is possible for the Mongolian cross-cultural missionary movement to ultimately become financially sustainable, one that is not dependent on outside sources but interdependent in partnership with others. As missiologist Howard Brant believes, "God has created every culture to be a missionary sending culture . . . we believe that God has placed workable systems within each culture that, when redeemed, enable mission to function" (2009, loc. 902).

While there are many facets to the theological diamond called mission, this dissertation assumes the premise that mission emanates from God's very person, plan, and character as revealed in Scripture (Ott, Strauss, and Tennent 2011, 56). Consequently, this dissertation acknowledges the following points.

As Moses attests, God is sovereign (Deut. 10:14 ESV).[7] Humanity, though made in God's image (Gen 1:26), rebelled and marred the relationship (Rom 3:23). Nevertheless, God's plan is one of redemption for all mankind meant to eventually establish God's kingdom on earth (Ott, Strauss, and Tennent 2011, 121; Wright 2010, 17).

With the birth, death, and resurrection of Jesus Christ, the Son of God as recorded in the gospels, there comes a significant development in God's plan of redemption. God the Father now defers all authority to the Son (Matt 28:19-20) and Jesus confers his given mission of reconciliation onto his followers (John 20:21). As Lesslie Newbigin suggests (1995, 65), the outpouring of the Holy Spirit on Jesus' followers in Acts 2 is perhaps the

---

[7] Unless otherwise stated, all Scripture references are from the English Standard Version of the Bible (ESV).

true birth place of the church as a missionary community now endowed with authority to complete the mission of God.

God provided the perfect circumstances and time that led to necessitating the moving out of the church from its Jerusalem centre out into the surrounding world (Acts 8:1) creating a vibrant centrifugal movement. This, in turn, created multiple centres for mission wherever communities of believers established themselves (Ott, Strauss, and Tennent 2011, 77).

Together with historian Stephen Neill (1986), this dissertation acknowledges several factors that enhanced the spread of Christianity. (i) Palestine sat within the Roman Empire with all the structural and societal advantages it offered. (ii) It was largely a Greek-speaking people to whom the gospel first went (30). (iii) Within the Roman Empire there were pockets of Jews, which gave the believing community a solid base from which to reach out (Acts 17:2, Rom 1:16). (iv) The Empire's mainly polytheistic societies had a hunger and curiosity concerning Christianity and the things of God (24-25). With signs, wonders, and miracles validating its authority (Acts 5:12), the church grew steadily, fulfilling the command of Jesus to go, make disciples of all nations (Matt 28:19-20).

Delimitations

The data gathering for this research was conducted between January and September 2020. The missionary participants in this study were determined with guidelines from Human Subject Research (HSR) concerns and were approved by Fuller Theological Seminary's HSR committee. Concerns for the physical safety and anonymity of the Mongolian missionaries interviewed for this study limited the sample to those cross-cultural missionaries who were able to attend a security training held in Chiang Mai, Thailand, in January 2020. At this point, conversations and interviews could, generally, be freely held.[8] As this training was conducted and organised by Pioneers, the sample was also confined to those on Pioneers teams or with some other field relationship to Pioneers. The sending church leaders were identified and chosen due to their direct connection to the selected cross-cultural missionaries.

While interviewees were primarily those with links to Pioneers, the application of results is not limited only to Pioneers. As an organisation, Pioneers is but one of several working together in Mongolia to see the Mongolian cross-cultural missionary movement established and strengthened. Nevertheless, it is fair to say that the results will most directly impact Pioneers' work as a missionary enabling organisation, yet acting as an example to those they interact with and work alongside in the context of Mongolia. In addition, several organisations are currently observing what Pioneers are doing and seeking to learn from their experience as a forerunner.

This study is limited to the Protestant churches in Mongolia. There are both Roman Catholic congregations and Russian Orthodox congregations within the Christian community at the time of writing, however I am unaware of any cross-cultural missionaries being sent from these churches. This study also excludes all cults and sects, including Jehovah's Witnesses, Mormons, and Baha'i, all of whom have active evangelistic programmes among the Mongolian people.

Limitations

I chose to conduct all the interviews and the two focus groups in the Mongolian language. I then had the interviews and focus group discussions transcribed and subsequently translated into English. Though being fluent in Mongolian allowed me to back-translate the transcripts for reliability purposes, I am not a native speaker; therefore, it is inevitable that, at times, small things and inferences will have been lost in translation.

---

[8] Refer to chapter 4 where the security issues are expanded upon.

Further, COVID-19 restrictions in Mongolia limited the ability to gather any formal follow up material, although there have been many informal conversations with participants throughout the dissertation period.

Dissertation Overview

Like the modern-day nation, the Mongolian church is relatively young and its growth and exposure to global influences over the past thirty years have left it struggling to find an authentic identity; as a result, it remains in a state of flux. Consequently, as a cross-cultural movement emerges out of the Mongolian church, it is imperative that this indigenous movement discover an authentic, contextually relevant and sustainable structure to build around. Accordingly, this research project sought to ask the pertinent questions: what might it take for the Mongolian church to develop a sustainable cross-cultural missionary movement, and what form might this movement take?

In seeking answers to this pertinent question this dissertation is organised into three parts. Part I explores the available precedent literature to discover some of the foundational core elements necessary for a strong missionary movement. Chapter 1 begins with the theological elements underpinning any missionary endeavour before examining the secular theory of movements and the necessary organisational structures and models. Chapter 2 evaluates examples of indigenous missionary movements from Africa, Asia, and Latin America, often referred to as the Global South or preferably, the Majority-World (Jenkins 2006, ix; Wan and Pocock 2009). Finally, in chapter 3, I attempt to paint a contextual portrait of Mongolia from a historical, socio-political and religious perspective before examining the Mongolian church and its current cross-cultural missionary movement within that context.

In part II, I describe my methodology for researching the current status of the Mongolian cross-cultural missionary movement (chapter 4) in a bid to discover the strengths and weaknesses of the movement. Then, in chapter 5, I discuss the findings, evaluate the state of the Mongolian cross-cultural missionary movement, its strengths and challenges, and presents four emerging themes.

Part III begins in chapter 6 with exploring how to implement changes based upon the findings of part II and develops a strategy for building a stronger and sustainable movement for the future together with the Mongolian Mission Partnership (MMP).[9] Finally, the conclusions and recommendations (chapter 7) will draw the whole dissertation together by presenting the conclusions of this study, suggesting recommendations and discussing the implications of this research project beyond Mongolia, practically and missiologically.

Summary

This introduction recognised that the Mongolian cross-cultural mission as a first-generation missionary movement. While passionate, it is young and struggling with identity, unity and sustainability. Therefore, this introduction proceeded to ask what it would take for the Mongolian church to develop a sustainable cross-cultural missionary movement and what form that movement might take. It continued by outlining the research design used to answer these questions. Thus, part I, begins this process by exploring the available and relevant precedent literature to discover the core elements necessary to a sustainable cross-cultural missionary movement.

---

[9] The Mongolian Mission partnership (MMP) is a newly formed association of leaders committed to supporting and strengthening the cross-cultural missionary movement (The Mongolian name is Монгол Илгээлтийн Хамтын Ажиллагааны Холбоо). While not being directly responsible for the formation of MMP, this research project and conversations leading to it together with the enforced COVID restrictions, seem to have been part of the catalyse toward the decision to form MMP.

Part I

Exploring Core Elements of a Cross-Cultural Missionary Movement

The current Mongolian cross-cultural missionary movement appears to be struggling under the weight of systems introduced by their Western and South Korean missionary partners, among other pressures. However, it is clear that one size does not fit all when it comes to missionary movements worldwide. Therefore, this literature review will explore available literature to discover core foundational elements necessary to establishing and sustaining a cross-cultural missionary movement. As well, I will investigate what has shaped twenty-first century missionary movements historically, and how it might apply to the burgeoning movement in Mongolia.

To accomplish this task, part I is divided into three chapters. Chapter 1 begins by focusing on the theological concept of the *missio Dei* and the church's role within the *missio Dei*. Once these foundations are laid, I present the theory of social movements and their operating organisations as a means for the *missio Dei* to be effectively carried out.

Chapter 2 explores examples of missionary movements from the Majority-World during the latter half of the twentieth century. As a Majority-World nation, Mongolia can gain valuable insight from these movements. Lastly, chapter 3 explores the cultural and historical context of the Mongolian cross-cultural missionary movement and the principles we might learn from the movement's progress so far.

Chapter 1

Fixed in God: The Rightful Place of Church and Mission

The Roman Emperor Constantine converted to Christianity in AD 312. This signalled the first significant shift in the church's understanding of mission as being rooted in God (Neill 1986, 41). During the ensuing time of popularity in Christianity and the growth of the institutionalised church, the understanding of mission altered to it being simply one of the tasks undertaken by the church rather than the reason and bedrock for its existence. Over the centuries of Christendom, tradition developed and argued for an ecclesiocentric understanding of mission. Yet, according to Wilbert Shenk, authentic mission needs to be theocentric to have a correct biblical understanding of mission (1999, 12). Mission needs to be God-centred. The following section focuses on the recapture in recent times of the true nature of mission, creating the necessary theological context for the Mongolian church's comprehension of mission.

From Ecclesiocentric Mission to a Theocentric Mission

Before leaping straight from the fourth century into the twentieth century's recapture of the true nature of mission, it is probably wise to briefly map the relationships between mission and the church through the intervening centuries. By doing so we can illuminate the pathway to what has been called the modern-day missionary movement.

The Church and Mission Relationship Through the Centuries

With the rise of Christianity as an official religion of the Roman Empire under Constantine, the idea of converting the heathen to anything other than an allegiance to Rome began to fade. Missiologist Ralph D. Winter suggests that, as a result, Christianity became ill-equipped to fulfil the great commission (Winter 2009a, 216). Succinctly put, Rome had tamed Christianity (Little 2002, 84).

Not content with the status quo, some began to drop out of church and society. Prior to Constantine, martyrdom was recognised as a probable cost of believing in Jesus as Lord. With this risk factor removed, some converts felt the need to put the cost back into following Christ. Hence Christians began to seek what missiologist Stephen Bevans calls "white martyrdom," that of an ascetic lifestyle, of Christian converts retreating into desolate places such as the desert (2002, 6). These individuals began to attract attention as others sought them out for spiritual guidance and inspiration; thus, monasticism became a way of life and a fresh witness to the world.[1]

Monastic communities grew through the ensuing centuries with many becoming less ascetic and more communal in their lifestyle and ministry to their surrounding environment. According to Bevans (6), these communities were a witness to civilisation and offered a semblance of normality in a world of war and incivility despite the turmoil of the times. Monasticism continued as a movement of God's people well into the next millennium and beyond.

The sixteenth century became the century of discovery by Christopher Columbus and other great explorers. It is also the century in which Martin Luther reportedly nailed his ninety-six theses to the door of the church in Wittenberg, Germany in 1517 (Marshall 2017, 12–13), signalling the Reformation and the break from Catholicism as the only true

---

[1] Stephen J. Davis, in his book *Monasiticism* (2018, 6) describes the Greek roots of the term and give five characteristics of monasticism as it developed during these centuries: solitude, the state of being set apart, withdrawal, community, and discipline.

church. These were tumultuous times as church fought church for power and dominion across continents, primarily causing an inward rather than outward missiological focus.

At the end of the eighteenth century, in 1792, Baptist minister William Carey, convicted of the responsibility of the church to mission, published a booklet entitled *An Enquiry into the Obligations of Christians to Use Means for the Conversion of the Heathen*. This booklet has been hailed as the beginning of the modern-day missionary movement with its outward focus on the nations, according to Winter (2009b, 264).

Towards the end of the nineteenth century another missionary pioneer, Hudson Taylor, sought a mission society willing to send missionaries to the interior of China. Unsuccessful in finding such a mission he eventually started the China Inland Mission in 1865 with friends. He drew and accepted missionary candidates from all denominations to evangelise the inland provinces, even against the railings of church leadership of the day (Huneycutt 2009, 378–79). While there are many other elements that kept the missionary zeal alive during ecclesiastic ownership of mission through the centuries, this period signalled the birth pangs of the modern-day missionary movement.

The Emergence of *Missio Dei* as the Centre of Mission

By the middle of the twentieth century a significant shift in missiological thinking concerning the foundational premise of mission began with a refocusing on God (Bosch 1991; Ott, Strauss, and Tennent 2011; Pocock, Van Rheenen, and McConnell 2005; Shenk 1999). According to missiologists Darrell L. Guder and Wilbert Shenk this shift was from the "ecclesiocentric" understanding of mission—the sense that mission is an activity undertaken by the church, acknowledged through the previous centuries—to a "theocentric" understanding of mission, where mission is recognised as an initiative of God rather than primarily an initiative of the church (Guder 1998, 4; Shenk 1999, 7).

Theologian and missiologist Lesslie Newbigin identifies the church as the "locus of mission." This is because the church bears witness to the nations concerning the good news of Jesus Christ. However, it is not the action of being his witness that is the beginning of mission. Instead, it is the presence of God's Holy Spirit within the community of believers that constitutes the real beginning (1989, 119). Mission, Newbigin argues, is the proclaiming of God's kingship over all things throughout history, and mission is the presence of God through the kingship of Jesus over the church. This he calls the "provenience of the kingdom" (1995, 64–65). While the church may be the locus of mission, the concept of mission itself originates in the Godhead (Rev. 7:10). Therefore, it is correct to identify mission as theocentric in nature and thus belonging to God: the *missio Dei* (the mission of God).

Historically, according to the South African missiologist David J. Bosch, the German theologian Karl Barth in a paper given in 1932 is credited as one of the first modern-day theologians to articulate mission as the activity of God (1991, 389). But it was not until the 5th International Missionary Conference at Willingen in 1952 following the aftermath of two world wars, the diminishing colonial world of empires, and a consequently crumbling and disillusioned Christendom, that mission was discussed as emanating from the very nature of the triune God. Unspoken, but in essence, the *missio Dei* (Bosch 1991, 390; Glasser and Engen 2003, 245).

In a more recent review of the World Mission Conferences[2] through the twentieth century, missiologist Wolfgang Gunther summarised the discussion thus, "Mission ultimately has its origin in God himself. God himself is the ground of mission .... So, mission is not founded on human intention, nor is the ... church the foundation of

---

[2] The International Missionary Conference (IMC) was a part of the World Mission Conferences (WMC) the first of which was Edinburgh 1910.

mission. Mission comes from God himself; the Church simply participates in that mission which remains, always, God's mission" (2003, 529).

In summary, within the worldwide church today, the term *missio Dei* is generally acknowledged theologically and biblically as the primary basis for the church's call to mission. Ott, Strauss, and Tennent expand this, stating,

> The Bible is from start to finish a missionary book, for it is the story of God himself reaching into human history to reconcile a fallen and rebellious humanity to himself and to reestablish his reign over all creation. In this sense God is a missionary God. (2011, Loc. 549)

Thus says theologian Christopher Wright, "The writings that now comprise our Bible are themselves the product of and witness to the ultimate mission of God" (2006, 48). This development forms a new missional hermeneutic with the God of the Bible at the centre of missionary movements: the *missio Dei*.

The Role of the Church in the *Missio Dei*

Establishing the *missio Dei* as the theological basis for the church's mission, the logical and natural conclusion is that God is a missionary God (Escobar 2003, 92; Bosch 1991, 372; Guder 1998, 4). Simply stated, God sent (*missio* meaning "to send") God's Son to bring salvation to the world (Jn 3:16), and Jesus sent the Holy Spirit to empower the church to continue that ministry (Acts 1:8). Thus, Jesus commissioned the church to be sent into the world (Jn 20:21). In doing so, the church becomes the primary agent, the locus of mission, for the continuation of God's mission given to Jesus (Ott, Strauss, and Tennent 2011, Loc. 200; Newbigin 1989, 119).

Missiologist Gregory Leffel observes that this is about the coming together of church and mission in what he describes as "church-in-mission or mission-church" (2007, 15). In contemporary missiology this thinking is encapsulated by the term "missional church" which declares that the church, at its core, is a missionary church (Kirk 2000, 30;

Bosch 1991, 372; Leffel 2007, 187; Guder 1998, 4). Leffel develops an eight-part framework to describe this relationship between church and mission, with parts four through eigth focusing on the church: (iv) The church is a movement mobilising believers to witness to God's reign in the world. (v) The church is a mediator, a body that furthers the work of redemption and salvation of man with God. (vi) The church is a grounded community, a living community acting together, Christ's body on earth. (vii) The church is gifted for mission and empowered by the Holy Spirit to engage the whole of humanity. (viii) The church is a sacrament of salvation, a sign of God's presence among God's people through the *missio Dei* (2007, chap. 2). Through this framework, the church and mission are eternally connected within the missionary nature of God. If church by its very nature should be missionary-minded then mission needs to be considered part of its DNA (Trebesch 2015, 54). Consequently, some argue that when mission-mindedness is lost or wanes, to the same degree does that church cease to be a church in a biblical sense. (Kirk 2000, 30; Newbigin 1965, 163).

In summary, following this pattern, the church's role in mission is identified as simply to be the instrument or agent of God's continuing salvation, made possible through the incarnation, death and resurrection of Jesus Christ. It has been sent out into the world to bring this good news to all creation until the end comes and Christ returns, the last phase of the mission of God. This brief review into the church's role in mission suggests the Mongolian church needs to consider the role of mission in its day to day life, and to consider how missional it is in its understanding and operation. The next section explores the mechanism and form of organisation the church might use to fulfil its God-given mission.

Forming and Sustaining a Movement

To determine and understand what defines a missionary movement it is necessary to understand the working of social movements and explore the correlation between them and missionary movements. While social movements are difficult to define succinctly, several definitions may help narrow the parameters for this study.

Sociologists Turner and Killian define social movements as "collectivity acting with some continuity to promote or resist a change in the society or organization of which it is a part" (1957, 223). Another definition from one of the originators of "movement theory," Herbert Blumer, states that social movements are

> collective enterprises seeking to establish a new order of life. They have their inception in a condition of unrest, and derive their motive power on one hand from dissatisfaction with the current form of life, and on the other hand, from wishes and hopes of a new system of living. (1986, 99)

From these two definitions, we note that people movements generally orient towards social change. Dissatisfied with the current status quo, the participants come together with a desire to establish a new order of life. This clarification is important as it means collective enterprises are more than just reactions to social situations, for reactions alone do not necessarily birth a movement. However, by seeking to establish an alternative or new order of life, there is purpose and movement towards a destination (Crossley 2002, 3).

The third definition by sociologists Donatella Della Porter and Mario Diani suggests social movements are:

- involved in conflict relations with clearly identified opponents
- linked by dense informal networks
- Share a distinct collective identity (2006, 20–21).

Together these three overlapping definitions build a multi-dimensional picture of a social movement. However, as the word movement suggests, healthy social movements will continue to evolve.

Collective Behaviour Theory

Perhaps the one common denominator in all social movements is that they function through some collective behaviour (Crossley 2002, 2; Della Porta and Diani 2006, 21; Blumer 1986, 99). Traditionally, collective behaviour theory focuses on movements emerging from unrest or dissatisfaction within any given situation as in Blumer's original definition above (1986, 99). While this is not wrong, it should not limit movements emerging for other reasons. For example, many early social movements of the twentieth century focused on nationalistic workers' rights, such as the right to fair pay or racial issues, such as the American civil rights movement. Today they tend to focus on environmental issues such as climate change or gender equality. Therefore, attempting to produce a simple, one-time definition of social movements is problematic.

While collective behaviour theories are not necessarily developed with a missiological perspective in mind, many of the elements of social movements are prevalent in missionary movements. They are collective enterprises with a common commitment and shared purpose in which the people involved desire to see social change and a new order of life emerge. As movements researcher Steve Addison observes, mission has "an agenda for change" (2011, 32).

Collective behaviour theories arose during the twentieth century; by the end of the century, according to sociologist Nida Kirmani, two major schools of thought emerged concerning social movements. Both appeared around the same time in the late 1960s early 1970s: Resource Mobilisation (RM) and New Social Movements (NSMs) (2008, 7).

Resource Mobilisation Theory (RM)

Resource Mobilisation (RM) theorists within the study of social movements believe the success of the movement depends primarily on resources (money, time, skills, etc.) and the ability to access them (Crossman 2019). As noted earlier, social movements traditionally centred on grievances and social or political conflict, both of which RM advocates argue are inherent in any society. Nevertheless, RM theorists recognise the need to form social movement organisations that can mobilise resources from potential donors directly to the issue at stake including potential donors outside the movement. Many missionary movements appear to operate along similar lines concerning finances and other resources.

New Social Movements (NSMs)

The other school of thought, New Social Movements (NSMs), came to the fore in a postmodern and post-industrialised era. Here, class distinctions blurred and merged due to the development of welfare systems and wider equal employment opportunities. NSMs, rather than struggling against the elitist or corporate conglomerates, rise out of struggles against social inequalities and against mass media-driven issues. Their ideology focuses on quality of life and lifestyle rather than economic redistribution. They advocate direct democracy, self-help groups and cooperative styles of social organisation (Pichardo 1997, 414). NSMs tend to operate outside the normal political channels and feed upon mobilising public opinion to gain leverage, often using well-ordered social disruption to make a point. An example in recent days is "Extinction Rebellion" which seeks change in government policies concerning climate change issues. According to their official website, at the core of Extinction Rebellion's philosophy is nonviolent civil disobedience. It states, "We promote civil disobedience and rebellion because we think it is necessary - we are asking people to find their courage and to collectively do what is necessary to bring about change" (Extinction Rebellion 2021).

NSMs are generally open to decentralised and non-hierarchical organisations, and are often anti-bureaucratic. Their participants tend to be marked by a common concern for the issue rather than any political cause. Because of these things some question the "newness" of such movements. Jean L. Cohen, professor of political thought at Columbia University, quoted by Pichardo, observes, "The old patterns of collective action certainly continue to exist in some movements they may even be statistically preponderant" (1997, 418). The Old Testament writer of the book of Ecclisiates would agree when he wrote, "there is nothing new under the sun" (Eccl 1:9).

Social movements may appear to change on the outside but the patterns of collective behaviour appear to run through both RM and NSMs. Attempting to place missionary movements within the world of social movements is not so easy as elements of both RMs and NSMs fit the profile of a missionary movement. Mission during the years of Christendom, approximately 1,500 years, largely blended cultural and sociopolitical reform with Christianity (i.e., the exporting of Western culture along with the gospel message, usurping the native culture and beliefs of the place or peoples concerned) (Nkomazana 2016, 30). Christianised nations were colonising and civilising those residing in the nations they entered. Whereas post-Christendom, in the twenty-first century, new movements are springing up more akin to NSMs in shape although not so radical in action, with a deliberate desire to see new life emerge into the cultures wherever the gospel is taken. New emerging missionary movements, especially from the Majority-World including countries like Mongolia, while being in nature less centralised and more informal, seeking to transform peoples from within socio-cultural settings still draw from the practices of each side of the social movement theory.

In summary, all movements appear to need a shared belief and a common concern, collectively acting as one. Of course, gleaning understanding from the secular world is all well and good, but the Christian perspective must be considered. Steve Addison, in his book *Movements that Changed the World* (2011), focuses on Jesus' mission and the simplicity of the movement he sought to establish away from any man-made structures. Movements, Addison declares, "change people, and changed people change the world" (2011, 29). He notes three simple realities to Jesus' movement: (i) the message, (ii) agenda for change, and (iii) conversion, where the new believers are committed to one another and drawn into the body of Christ in a local church community (32). Addison also identifies five characteristics he believes are found in every dynamic missionary movement:

  i)   white-hot faith,
  ii) commitment to the cause,
  iii) contagious relationships,
  iv) rapid mobilization, and
  v)   adaptive models (22-25).

Similarly, missiologist Howard Brant defines seven essential elements of such a movement from the Majority-World:

  i)   Called Individuals
  ii) Visionary Leaders
  iii) Missional Churches
  iv) Appropriate Training
  v)   Flexible Structures
  vi) Sustainable Finances
  vii) Powerful Prayer Movements (Brant 2009).

First, Brant likens called individuals to bulldozers because he believes nothing will stop them, and it is those who are called who enable emerging mission movements to become truly active. They are the beginning of a movement (loc. 739), says Brant. Second, visionary leaders ask the questions: What binds us together? What tears us apart? How do we work together? (Rickett 2014, loc. 370). Third, the church must have a missional heart. That mission is found in its DNA composition. As Brant comments, a missional church is "outwardly focused and ministers cross-culturally into the non-Christian world" (2009, loc. 799). Fourth, Brant highlights that training should be solidly biblical, contextualised for the Majority-World and for the need of practical skills to enable missionaries to be self-sustaining in part (loc. 844). Fifth, structures need to be simple and remain flexible, taking into account "the cultural diversity of a global missions movement" (loc. 882). Sixth, probably the most challenging, is sustainable finances; however, Brant believes that "God has created every culture to be a missionary sending culture." Therefore, God must have placed within that culture the means to finance God's work of mission (loc. 903). While partnerships with other wealthier nations and established international missionary movements might be necessary for the early days of movements from the Majority-South, prolonged availability of such support can cripple the local churches in their missionary vision and involvement. Mongolian missionaries today can attest that long term financial dependence is not ideal nor sustainable. Ultimately, entrepreneurial skills are needed among the Mongolians if the work is to be sustained long-term. Finally, seventh, none of this will happen without powerful prayer undergirding the whole movement. Prayer has always preceded the moving of God. From those patiently waiting in prayer in the upper room when the Holy Spirit fell on the first followers of Jesus (Acts 2:1-4) to modern-day revivals such as the Hebridean revival of the 1950s (Peckham et al. 2004) prayer has been the foundation of powerful movements in mission.

Organisational Elements

Today there is an acceptance that organisations act as carriers for social movements (Zald and McCarthy 1987, 1), although, as Addison observes, they are not the totality of a movement (2011, 28). However, movements often consist of various organisations that share the movement's common purpose. For instance, the modern peace movement consists of many organisations like Greenpeace[3] or groups like the Network of Christian Peace Organisations.[4] In order to glean possible lessons from organisational literature that can be applied to missions movements, it is essential and practical to consider both large and small organisational structures, both Non-Government Organisations (NGOs) and those within the business world.

In its simplest form those who study organisations concentrate on structures, goals and personnel within any given organisation to analyse it and consider its efficiency. While being reductive these three elements provide a focal point for studying precedent literature on organisations and consider how these aspects might be applied to the creation of a missionary organisation or network. Before this, however, one of the significant bonds within any organisation is the organisational culture. The culture gives identity and cohesiveness to the organisation. Culture influences and connects with every stratum of an organisation and will be considered before returning to the three basic elements: structure, goals, and personnel.

Organisational Culture

At a general level, missionary anthropologist Paul Hiebert defined culture generally as "the more or less integrated systems of ideas, feelings, and values and their associated patterns of behaviour and products shared by a group of people who organise and regulate what they think, feel and do" (1985, 30). Hence, we understand that culture

---

[3] www.grenpeace.org.uk
[4] www.ncpo.org.uk/about-the-ncpo

is always a collective phenomenon; it is about the unwritten rules we live by and derive from our social life. In their seminal work, *Cultures and Organizations*, Hofstede, Hofstede, and Minkov (2010) describe four layers of the cultural onion: symbols, heroes, rituals, and the deepest and often unseen level of values evident in an organisation's practices.

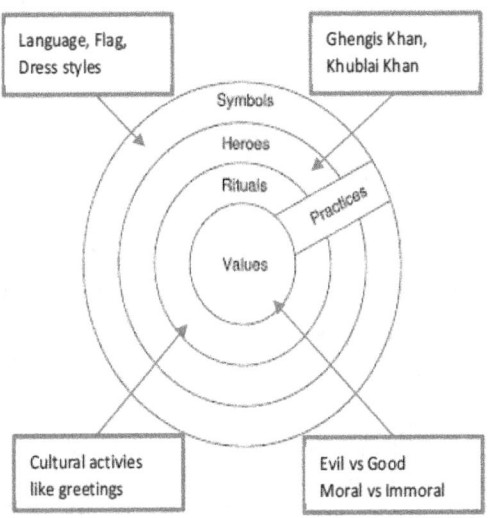

Figure 1: The Cultural Onion
(adapted from Hofstede, Hofstede, and Minkov 2010, 8)

At an organisational level of culture, Hofstede et al. distinguish between national and organisational cultures describing national culture as the mental software imparted during our formative years in family and school. In contrast, organisational cultures are acquired when we enter the workplace or organisation, primarily constituting the organisation's work practices (2010, 346). Organisational theorist Edgar Schein identifies these practices or behaviours as "the shared basic assumptions that evolve about how things should be done, how the mission is to be achieved, how goals are to be met"

(2017, 158). In summary, the organisational culture becomes the core element of who they are and how they will act to achieve their organisational goals.

Structure, Goals, and Personnel

To explore further elements of successful organisations, I now return briefly to the three main aspects of analysis; structure, goals, and personnel, beginning with organizational structure.

Structure

From the plethora of definitions available for the concept of structure, we can determine that an organisational structure is a system that guides the activities of an organisation towards achieving its purpose and goals. In an article in *Harvard Business Review* "Hierarchy and Network: Two Structures, One Organization" (2011), leadership consultant John Kotter recognises that many traditional structures are centralised with clear hierarchical leadership and design, and have been around since the beginning of the last century. However, he concludes that these traditional systems may not survive the pace of change required to be competitive in the twenty-first century. Consequently, a growing number of decentralised structures or networks are emerging in today's business world. These systems are more egalitarian, team-based, and more of an adaptive network that suits the current transformative climate (2011).

Goals

An organisation's goals are the objectives, the whys and wherefores of achieving those objectives. Sociologist P. G. Aquinas succinctly states that "goals are the reason for an organization's existence and the outcomes it seeks to achieve" (2009, 86). In the business world the acronym SMART has been associated with the discussion of goals, which are to be: Specific, Measurable, Achievable, Realistic, and Time-bound (Doran, Miller, and Cunningham 1981). SMART has been a useful tool to consider goal setting within organisations ever since. Without such simple formulas goals can often have a tendency to miss the mark. An example of this would be the Mongolian missionary movement's 10/20 goal.[5] While it was specific and time-bound, it might not have been realistic and measurable at the time of conception. Little thought had been given to strategy and how it might be achieved.[6]

Personnel

Numerous scholars agree that strong dynamic leadership is essential when establishing any new entity (Schein 2017; Kraemer 2015; Butler 1994; Altland 2015). Schein believes strong leaders will set the initial organisational culture in as much as they are self-confident and determined, which leads to strong assumptions concerning the environment they will operate in and their clear sense of their role (2017, 106). In choosing the environmental context of the mission, founder-leaders will then be responsible for recruiting the necessary personnel to form the best team to achieve their purposes (Schein 1985, 106). Therefore, within the Mongolian cross-cultural missionary movement, it would seem essential for organisations and agencies to have strong, charismatic leaders with clear goals and trajectories who seek to cement healthy relationships with those tasked with meeting the requirements of the goals.

In more recent times, a structure called boundaryless organisation has emerged. It was a term initially coined at General Electric sometime in the late 1980s and early 1990s when the company were seeking to improve and streamline operations, attempting to

---

[5] The 10/20 goal was established in 2009 and aimed at reaching 10 percent of Mongolia and its diaspora with the gospel by 2020.

[6] During 2020 there were a number of meetings held by Mongolian Evangeical Alliance to ask what went wrong and how might the Monoglian church learn from the failure to meet the expected target in order to set further goals in the future.

reduce bureaucracy while gaining efficiency (Ashkenas et al. 2002, xx). Theoretically, it is a framework for streamlining procedures and enhancing performance in a changing world.

Traditional organisational structures often divide their responsibilities across four common boundaries: vertical, those between different levels of people; horizontal, usually between the organisation's functions and disciplines; external, those between the organisation and the outside world; geographical, those between the various locations connected with the organisation (2).

Boundaryless organisations challenge these traditional patterns and seek ways of allowing information and ideas to permeate these usually impenetrable boundaries, or departments, creating a free flow of initiatives across all levels. Traditionally, boundaries have helped to keep tasks and responsibilities distinct. Consequently, boundaryless thinking does not seek to remove them; instead, it aims to see them become more organic and permeable, allowing a flow that enables an organisational structure to function as a team (3). This flexibility brings a greater egalitarian approach to organisations, something Asian hierarchical cultures such as Mongolian traditional culture may find challenging.

Clearly a wealth of material is available to help shape and structure an organisation. However, the majority deal with professional companies or NGOs often functioning with paid staff and skilled labour. The question raised is whether this material can be applied to missionary organisations which are traditionally staffed with volunteers. Organisational strategist Barry Atland, in his book *Engaging The Head, Heart and Hands of a Volunteer* (2015), considers organisations from that volunteer standpoint. He observes that every organisation needs defined elements of what he terms; vision, mission, values and competencies (loc. 784), believing every organisational leader has a responsibility to grapple with these four basic elements. This is his V-M-V-C model (loc. 795).

Simply put, the vision states the direction, and the mission is the roadmap to reach the destination. Next, the values define the character traits of those within the organisation, and the competencies define what the personnel should do to accomplish the mission. Leaders use these four elements to intentionally create the culture and become a primary guideline for membership and evaluating performance within a volunteer organisation. Atland states, "by leveraging the V-M-V-C, leaders reinforce a clearly defined culture and purpose" (loc. 834). Volunteerism is still a new thought in Mongolian society where many require finances just to survive day to day causing them to seek salaried positions. From a mission perspective finding those who will regularly give of their time to help with simple, practical tasks without pay is currently rare.

In summary, we observe that organisations benefit from dynamic leaders with clear vision and purpose and who are able to engage suitable personnel. Structuring the organisation around clear goals and setting an organisational culture that will steer the whole operation are essential elements to success. Secular literature naturally dispenses with the role of Scripture or the rightful place of God within the organisation; however, these principles are clearly defined and work with both secular and church-based organisations.

Sustainable Elements

It will take more than a well-organised missionary movement from Mongolia to sustain the long-term pursuit of its goals. Mongolia is a relatively spacious country, approximately 1,500,000 km^2 yet sparsely populated with a little over 3,300,000 people (United States Government, Central Intelligence Agency 2022). Therefore, any missionary movement or single entity from a church that only represents 1.2 percent of the population (Visser, Byambatseren, and Stephens 2019, 8) will need support and cooperation not only from the various sending agencies and churches within the country but also from the broader church across the globe. With this in mind, the following section will briefly consider sustainability through the lenses of partnerships and networks.

Partnerships

Partnership as a missiological term is relatively new even though the concepts are as old as the Bible itself. For the purposes of this study, Luis Bush, former president of Partners International, gives the clearest definition of partnership, stating that it is "an association of two or more autonomous bodies that have formed a trusting relationship and fulfil agreed-upon expectations by sharing complementary strengths and resources, to reach their mutual goal" (Bush and Lutz 1990, 46). While Luis Bush and Lorry Lutz identify ten elements of partnerships within this statement in their book *Partnering in Ministry*, three stand out when considering the Mongolian cross-cultural missionary movement: (i) a mutual goal: the importance of a clear agreed-upon goal of the partnership, (ii) autonomous bodies: all parties are equal, but also complementary, and (iii) sharing of resources in order to achieve the desired goal of reaching the Mongol diaspora with the gospel (1990).

Biblically, the Trinity is understood to exemplify how a Christian partnership should operate. In *Church and Mission Agencies Together* (2017), Ivan Liew concludes that partnership is integral to the nature of God. The oneness of the Father, Son, and Holy Spirit is marked by their distinct roles and interdependence, displaying a unique relationship of mutuality (loc. 654). As missiologist William Taylor writes, "God dwells in community" (1994, 15). There is a unity in this mutuality as Jesus states, "that they may all be one, just as You, Father, are in me, and I in You, that they also may be in us" (Jn 17:21). Ecclesiastes reminds us that while two are better than one, "a threefold cord is not quickly broken" (Eccl 4:19-10).

Mutuality and equality, the working together towards a common goal, are foundational to successful partnerships. If these two elements are established, then the sharing of resources will slowly follow. Missionary movements from small countries and even smaller churches have a tendency to protect the resources each church or agency may hold. However, when mutual acceptance and trust are achieved sharing those resources should become more manageable.

When partnerships develop between Majority-World mission movements and other missions, especially in the Western world, experience has shown that these partnerships are not straightforward (Butler 1994; Tan 2011). Head of VisionSynergy, Philip Butler, in his book *Kingdom Partnerships in The '90s: Is There a Way Forward?* (1994) highlights some of the tensions that arise from such partnerships. He observes cultural differences, communication challenges, financial issues and personality conflict (16). He comments that Westerners have been influenced by their individualistic culture and worldview influencing how they understand and believe Christianity operates. Yet, the community is the place of accountability, checks and balances. In the individualistic world, calling and vision, for instance, can often go unchecked (16). Ultimately, Butler considers that individualism without accountability can distort our mission strategy and practice. Recognising that in traditional cultures, "the deepest values are tied up in community," he believes the church must instead offer an alternative community that is at least equal, if not better, than their current community (16).

Like organisations, partnerships still need dynamic individuals or leaders, those with vision and passion, for "without people of vision and commitment partnerships perish." Consequently, partnerships take time to develop and need well-defined goals, objectives, and perseverance, which are better understood in community (28-29). Cross-cultural partnerships, especially between Western and Majority-World nations like Mongolia, will take some working out.

As a result motivation for the partnership is crucial. Each party must be willing to consider how they might benefit from their partnership. Butler suggests benefits could include: (i) recognising and utilising each other's strengths, (ii) working together reduces many of the risks involved in going it alone, (iii) the unity of groups working together towards a common goal is attractive to outside donors, and (iv) a sense of longevity that partnerships can bring to mission can be achieved (19–20). Partners need to be clear from the beginning, coming on equal terms and knowing with clarity what each other brings to the partnership and articulating how one will benefit from this partnership.

In his book *Making Your Partnership Work* (2014), Majority-World partnership expert Daniel Rickett focuses on two interdependent relationships: joint ventures and complementary partnerships (loc. 347). Partnerships, he contends, divide into three sections covering: vision, relationship, and results (loc. 353). Each segment acts as a wide-angle lens, giving a view of each segment's small components giving nine smaller components (see figure 2 below taken from the book). Each of these, he would argue, is necessary to successful partnerships (loc. 366).

It is noteworthy that most authors writing about cross-cultural partnerships focus on partnerships between the Majority-World and the Western world (Maxwell 1999; Hackett 2010; Livermore 2010; Rickett 2000). Such partnerships are necessary and significant for Mongolian mission agencies and churches to consider, especially in their infancy. However, we need to consider the local partnerships across agencies and churches involved in mission within Mongolia. In these instances, parameter shifts need to be explored. For example, many cultural challenges and language differences are potentially eased, at least until mission field experiences challenge the individual missionaries. Negatively, it is also true that the legacies of socialism make mutual trust difficult for Mongolians. Therefore, studying and discussing the benefits, practicalities, and challenges of such joint ventures, both within Mongolia and with external partners, is essential to long-term sustainability.

VISION	Shared vision	What has God invited us to do together?
	Compatibility	What binds us together? What could tear us apart?
	Ground Rules	How do we work together?
RELATIONSHIP	Alliance Champions	Who is responsible to make it work?
	Cross-Cultural Understanding	What cultural difficulties may help or hinder the relationship?
	Mutual Trust	What gives us confidence in each other?
RESULTS	Meaningful Results	What difference will it really make in the work of the gospel?
	Documentation	How do we keep track of agreements, contributions, and outcomes?
	Learning and change	How do we handle changes, opportunities, and disappointments?

Figure 2 The Imperatives of Partnership Design
(Rickett 2014, loc. 370)[7]

Networks

Networks are a looser grouping of like-minded entities, which Butler describes as "any group of individuals or organisations sharing a common interest, who regularly communicate with each other to enhance *their individual purposes*" (Butler 2005, 34). For instance, Global Connections is a UK based network of churches and agencies with a passion for mission.[8] Similarly, many larger countries and continents appear to have

---

[7] Used with the author's permission.
[8] www.globalconnections.org.uk

established mission networks. This causes one to consider how mission networks can ultimately benefit the Mongolian mission community and how they need to be structured.

The Mongolian Evangelical Alliance (MEA), until recently, was the only body or network available to the whole Mongolian church.[9] MEA is a member of the Asian Evangelical Alliance (AEA), a regional participant of the World Evangelical Alliance (WEA). AEA describes its purpose is to

> Promote and nurture unity, collaborations and co-operation among ministry organizations, church networks and primarily the National Evangelical Alliances within Asia and with those outside Asia for the purpose of building, strengthening and expanding the Kingdom of God in Asia and beyond. (Asian Evangelical Alliance 2018)

Its vision and purposes appear too all-encompassing, making it more of an umbrella organisation than a hands-on effective network. Initially, it is useful for nations like Mongolia to become members of AEA; however, while it may give global recognition through the WEA, it is too broad to impart influence or guidance at a more local level.

The Korean World Mission Association (KWMA)[10] is worth considering as a more practical model for Mongolia. Established in 1990, KWMA's vision and mission statements are simple; bringing a sense of oneness and community to its members, which is critical in an Asian cultural setting. Yet mission remains the core of this network as their mission statement says, "We are committed to finishing the remaining task of missions by co-operation and unity" ("Korean World Mission Association" 2017).

East Asia has very few networks like COMIBAM[11] in Latin America or the India Missions Association in India (IMA); two of the collaborations to be reviewed in chapter 2. Nevertheless, significant numbers of Mongolian missionaries and churches are affiliated with denominations or international organisations like Youth With a Mission

---

[9] In later chapters the Monoglian Mission Partnership (MMP) emerges as another potential such network that seeks to serve the whole church.

[10] www.kwma.or.kr

[11] COMIBAM is the English acronym for *Congreso Misionero IberoAmericano*

(YWAM) or Campus Crusade (Cru).[12] However, these are basically cross-cultural partnerships under the organisational banner at best; national groups subsumed into the international structure of a larger organisation.

Seventy years of Soviet socialism have left Mongolians hesitant to trust each other; hence a willingness, even desire, to partner with Western or Korean missions and churches appears more inviting. While this is true it has been suggested that initial partnerships with these organisations can potentially create the environment and experience necessary to foster the growth and development of an indigenous partnership.

Summary

I have briefly explored in this chapter some of the essential elements of forming and sustaining a cross-cultural missionary movement from Mongolia. I have established a theological premise for mission in the words of Jesus to his followers "as the Father has sent me, so I send you" (John 20:21), identifying mission as emanating from and belonging to God, the *missio Dei,* rather than being something that the church undertakes. Therefore, mission is to be theocentric not ecclesiocentric in its understanding. I also highlighted the integral and rightful role of the church as God's chosen community, God's primary agent in fulfilling God's mission. In light of this discussion, this research seeks to discover how much the Mongolian church fully grasps and understands the mission of God and its role in that mission, and to further disover if mission is part of the church's DNA.

Practically, I considered the necessary organisational elements required for movements, such as the Mongolian cross-cultural missionary movement, to enable it to function effectively within society and the wider world. As a small nation and even smaller church, this movement will need to consider partnerships within Mongolia and

---

[12] www.ywam.org; www.cru.org

the international mission community. Partnership opportunities and wider networks that are available to this growing movement, and what might they look like are questions to be raised through this research. I will explore in chapter 2 some examples of mission movements from the Majority-World to discover valuable contextual lessons applicable to the Mongolian cross-cultural missionary movement.

Chapter 2

Majority-World Indigenous Missionary Movements

According to researchers Zurlo, Johnston, and Crossing (2020), at the beginning of the twentieth century there were around 62,000 missionaries taking the good news of Jesus Christ into the world. By 2020 that figure was reckoned to be nearer 420,000 (17). Yet, by the beginning of the twenty-first century, the percentage of the world's population identified as Christian (32.4 percent) was actually lower than at the beginning of the twentieth century, when it was purported to be at 34.5 percent (9). However, these researchers predict that by 2050 the percentage of Christians will significantly increase,

> The decline of Christianity in the Global North is now being outpaced by the rise of Christianity in the Global South (i.e., Africa, Asia, Latin America, Oceania). Christians in sub-Saharan Africa generally have high birth rates, and people from other religions continue to convert to Christianity in China, India, Cambodia, Mongolia, and elsewhere throughout Asia. (9)

As the centre of global Christianity shifts from the North to the South, we see declining numbers of missionaries sent out from the North and an increase in missionaries sent out from the Majority-World (Global South) (Johnson et al. 2013, 76). Today this same report suggests nine of the top twenty mission-sending nations are, in fact, in the Majority-World (76).

I use the term indigenous in this chapter to imply contextual relevancy. Historically the term indigenous has been a botanical label; for instance, trees that are said to be indigenous to certain regions or countries of the world (Terry and Payne 2013, 105). However, in terms of the church it has only been applied since the middle of the nineteenth century, primarily by two men developing different strategies on opposite sides of the Atlantic Ocean: Henry Venn (1796-1873) and Rufus Anderson (1796-1880) (Kim 2009, loc. 507).

These movements sought to establish churches in locations that were self-supporting, self-governing and self-propagating (Terry and Payne 2013, 105), birthing and identifying what some call indigenous churches. In like manner, the term indigenous can be applied to missionary movements as well as to churches. Therefore, this study will refer to missionary movements as being indigenous, meaning contextualised and culturally relevant and potentially sustainable.

This chapter will examine different examples of Majority-World indigenous missionary movements and show the importance of partnerships through these regional snapshots. I will show that when there is encouragement towards developing contextual theology, provision of adequate training for cross-cultural missionaries, commitment to prayer and financial investment from the local church, and the development of strategic partnerships, these movements have the potential to flourish. I will offer examples from three different regions of the world: (i) Africa, (ii) Asia, and (iii) Latin America. Much of the available literature is in case study form rather than academic research and contains a significant historical content, resulting in the arguments being of a more practical and reflective nature, as many are movements in motion, changing in a changing world.

African Missionary Movements

In this section, I observe how a nation's history influences the church culturally and the importance of untangling the *missio Dei* from the confusion of those influences to discover a true contextual identity for mission.

To grasp the complexity of mission in Africa in the twenty-first century, it is essential to understand the context from which modern-day Africa was born: the Berlin conference of 1884/85. During this conference the colonial political powers, mainly of Europe, came together over a three-month period and decisively partitioned off the African continent for the convenience of their own economic gains. Partitioning was accomplished without African representation and without considering historical, tribal or cultural traditions (Akinwumi 2008, 9). Thus many issues challenging the African continent today are arguably rooted in the Berlin conference's decisions. This action was also to have a marked effect on Christianity within Africa.

Nigerian historian Olayemi Akinwumi notes that mission efforts within Africa prior to this conference were largely cooperative across the continent (12). After partitioning, the various mission movements and organisations which previously operated collectively, separated into their different national and cultural denominations, such as Anglicans with the British or Catholics with the French. Denominational independence began, and for the most part, churches and missions simply became socioeconomic pawns in the political games of the colonisers, dismantling any previous sense of harmony in the missionary movement. Partitioning was not only on a socioeconomic level but also became spiritual, institutionalising the church (10). This brief background sheds light on how a nation's history influences every level of social life including the church.

Emerging Missionary Movements

Through the tumultuous years of the twentieth century indigenous Christian missions began emerging out of Africa, initially through the newly forming African Independent Churches (AICs). Akinwumi (2008) comments that these churches were "largely a reaction to European domination of Church leadership. They were also a reaction to how Europeans disdained the African way of life." These indigenous churches signified the beginning of what is known as the Africanising of Christianity (16; see also

Talla 2009, loc 2871). Through the remaining turbulent twentieth century, Africa experienced the diminishing and dismantling of colonialism and the beginning of independence for many partitioned nations. The challenge for these young countries was to begin to untangle themselves from the influence of colonisation and to rediscover and rebuild their African cultural identity in the modern world. This rebuilding included Christianity rediscovering its true African identity and the Africanising of the *missio Dei*.

African Christianity specialist Matthew Ojo observes that there was "tremendous progress in African missionary enterprises all over the continent and among the migrated Africans in the West, as a result of the Pentecostal and Charismatic Renewal" (1997, 538). Thus the 1970s experienced a huge rise in national initiatives mobilising Africans into mission, with the first recorded indigenous African interdenominational mission sending agency being formed in Nigeria in 1975. Today African cross-cultural missionaries operate in over sixty-five countries worldwide (Olonade 2009, 371).

With this as a background, the following two examples may seem an unusual choice to some missiologists but have been chosen as they resonate with some of the situations the Mongolian missionary movement is tackling concerning culture and context. Both highlight the challenges facing foreign missionaries to Africa or, in this instance, Mongolia when involved with emerging indigenous missionary movements.

First, the Church of Pentecost in Ghana (CoP) highlights the process of contextualisation and the struggles when a movement begins expanding across the world. Second, the *Rukwadzano* women's movement, while not strictly a cross-cultural missionary movement, reflects the issues raised through organisational and denominational influences upon indigenous Christian movements. *The Unwritten Text: The Indigenous African Women's Movement in Zimbabwe* (Nyajeka 2006) is written from the perspective and understanding of the African women involved in this movment's beginning. It also highlights some of the issues of culture clash and the importance of indigenisation in the effectiveness and sustainability of a national movement.[1]

Ghana: The Church of Pentecost (CoP)

One movement that typifies the rise of missionary enterprises from Africa is the Church of Pentecost (CoP) whose roots trace back to the British missionary James Mckeown, who arrived in Ghana in 1937. CoP's website states that as of 2019 there were over 3,400,000 members, and it currently works in 105 different countries (Church of Pentecost 2021). Ghanaian theologian Opoku Onyinah believes the success of CoP through its various stages is due to Mckeown's contextualising methods, noting that

> First, he accepted the Ghanaian concept of the Onyankopong (the Supreme Being) . . . . Second, McKeown accepted the Ghanaian worldview of malevolent and benevolent spirits; he preached that receiving the Holy Spirit as evidenced by speaking in tongues meant that nothing would hurt the person, even in evangelization . . . . Third, he accepted the Ghanaian belief in life after death . . . . Fourth, he showed his trust not only in God but also in Ghanaians by saying that they could do without the help of white men or other evangelists. This was sowing the seed of an indigenous church (2004, 222).

McKeown allowed them to preach and interpret the Scriptures through Ghanaian eyes and only corrected misperceptions when necessary (222). He also appears to have been influenced by the three-self movement, developed around a century earlier (236). He allowed God to draw them together into communities (self-propagating). He encouraged each member to bring tithes and offerings from whatever resources God had given, rather than seeking funding from outside (self-supporting). Eventually, however, as the church grew and multiplied, a centralised, more formal organisational structure

---

[1] Farai David Muzorewa wrote a chapter entitled "Through Prayer to Action: The Rukwadzano Women of Rhodesia" in *Themes in the Christian History of Central Africa* (1975), from the Church's perspective. I however, am interested in how the Zimbabwean women perceived the situation in order to help with understanding the Mongolian perspective of their cross-cultural mission movement as a Westerner.

was established (self-governing) bringing its members accountability, discipline, and security—something that Onyinah considered suited the Ghanaian culture of the time (223).

Initially, CoP spread through migration as individuals began moving through West African countries. More recent decades saw the arrival of Ghanaians in the West together with their worship styles, preaching, and forms of church. For the Christians one of the primary motivators in mission was the belief in the imminent return of Christ, giving them a sense of urgency to share the gospel (228). Another strength was the orality of the culture, sharing theology and social values through storying rather than lectures or schooling. Soon the church in Ghana recognised the need for a structure to coordinate the activities of all those who had gone out and an International Missions Office was formed (229).

One point of note is the struggle these migrants experienced in owning their cultural identity when immersed in Western cultures. As a result, many retreated into forming CoP churches among their own in their new location suggesting perhaps a difficulty in cultural adaptation. Thus, they were unsuccessful in reaching the Western nations for Christ through the diasporic community as they had first desired and were unable to meet their own needs within the Western churches (228-29). Onyinah suggests that it was partly due to an underdeveloped mission theology within the church and the strong influence of McKeown's ideas on centralising the organisation (240).

This picture of the CoP and its mission work suggests the importance for the Mongolian church to develop a good theology of mission and to learn to understand its own cultural influences as they travel cross-culturally.

Zimbabwe: *Rukwadzano*

Another movement giving insight into the complexities of developing an African indigenous movement is the story of the indigenous women's movement emerging from Zimbabwe (formerly Rhodesia) during the twentieth century: *Rukwadzano*. While not a missionary movement per se, it is an indigenous African movement from the former Rhodesia and part of the United Methodist Mission.[2] This account is interesting because the perspective under discussion is from an African woman's understanding, taken from some of those involved in the movement's early days (Nyajeka 2006, 19).

According to Tumani Nyajeka, *Rukwadzano's* humble beginnings were bathed in prayer as eight pastors' wives came together to gather wood and pray as they did so (21). Out of concern for these unofficial meetings the Western missionary women on a small mission station initiated a Bible study and sought to teach the local women the Scriptures, specifically teaching them how to become Bible-women and wives to their future church-leader husbands; literally, how to be godly housewives from a foreign colonial perspective (160). There was nothing malicious in this approach from the Western missionaries. It simply reflected their interpretation and understanding of Scripture through their Western colonial eyes of the day.

As time progressed there was an evident clash of cultures and worldviews. In bringing literacy to the Manyika women the missionaries inadvertently gave opportunity for these women to interpret for themselves the things they were reading in the Scriptures. Outwardly, the movement grew within the United Methodist Church and became an official organisation. But inwardly, an indigenous women's movement was being shaped by their own African worldview and understanding of Scripture until, in a free Zimbabwe, their contextualised message found a true home as the leaders found independence (161-62). Today *Rukwadzano* is influencing women across Africa because,

---

[2] www.umnews.org/en/news/celebrating-womens-movement-at-historic-prayer-hill

according to Nyajeka, these women had learnt "the essence of the Christian faith and translated it into their traditional culture" (24).

In the twenty-first century we understand much more about cultural worldviews and the process of contextualisation and appreciate, with some personal shame, the influences of colonialism. However, this brief foray into the *Rukwadzano* from an insider's perspective shows us how much our own culture can influence our interpretation of Scripture, along with the importance of having a more humble egalitarian approach to expatriate missionary involvement. Therefore, learning from the *Rukwadzano* movement, we might see that indigeneity within the Mongolian cross-cultural missionary movement needs to be led by the Mongolians and gently corrected only when necessary by those supporting them if we are to see a truly sustainable and indigenous movement.

Summary

Briefly assessing both of these movements as representative of how God has been moving across Africa, Paul Hiebert is rightly reflects that, "Most mission movements have led to theological crises" (1985, 196). Hiebert considers that it takes approximately three or four generations in a new church environment before these movements are able to absorb and consider theology for themselves (196). Therefore, it is important to acknowledge that each culture and people should read Scripture through their own eyes and be able to make application accordingly, though this process may take three or four generations.

Perhaps the biggest challenge across Africa has been the strength with which Western colonial missionary influence has held sway. Mongolia may not have experienced colonialism and Christendom in the same manner. Yet, the overbearing presence of communism and the uncontextualised reach of the early missionaries in the 1990s created similar control issues. Western missionaries have extensive experience, but often the confidence it can give has the potential to hinder rather than encourage emerging movements. It is important to provide the nationals space to identify what shape or form an indigenous missionary movement might take. Both of the above movements developed independent African interpretations making the message of the Scriptures relevant and applicable.

Finally, Africans traditionally have a strong spiritual component to their lives, enabling them to embrace the rise of Pentecostalism through the last century and the role of the Holy Spirit within the church; healings and miracles are regular elements of African Christianity (Haar 2003, 411–12). This spiritual core has aided the missionary movement within the African churches.

African indigenous movements are now moving into what Hiebert (1985) labels the third and fourth generation, and out of the church are emerging some significant theologians. Africanisation of Christianity is becoming a reality and a strength. Mongolians experience a similar spiritual and cultural climate, yet this review considers whether the Mongolia church will need to wait for three or four generations before their movements are truly indigenised. As well, the issues of the importance of self-theologising to the true indigenisation process and the place that the availability of global technology and the internet play in shrinking this time frame for Majority-World nations like Mongolia must be examined. The development of a sound theology of mission within the church is important to aiding sustainability.

Asian Missionary Movements

While it is possible to talk of Asian Missionary Movements (AMMs) on the one hand, on the other, Asia as a continent (like Africa) covers many different nations, peoples and cultures as far apart as India and Korea or China and Pakistan. Therefore, simply speaking of AMMs could overlook the distinctives of each national missionary movement if confined under one banner (Tan 2011, 52). Attentive to this aspect and observing the proximity of Korea to Mongolia and its significant involvement in mission to Mongolia, this section will focus primarily on the Korean Missionary Movement (KMM). I will then briefly consider a Singapore church's model and the more general characteristics of other Asian Missionary Movements (AMMs).

The Korean Missionary Movement (KMM)

This section will consider how the church growth and missionary movement of South Korea since its formation has had an affinity with Mongolia's more recent history, thus offering many positive and cautionary lessons.

Explosive Growth

Missiologist Julie Ma (2011, 78) observes that during the last quarter of the twentieth century the South Korean church (hereafter referred to as the Korean church) experienced great spiritual and physical blessing, and since the 1970s the KMM has grown rapidly. At the Korean World Mission Conference in 2018 it was reported that there were now 27,993 Korean missionaries serving in more than 171 countries (KWMA 2019). With a continued increase at a rate of around 2000 a year, J. Ma estimates there will be over 100,000 Korean missionaries by 2030, confirming Korea as the second-largest missionary-sending country in the world (J. Ma 2011, 78). The strengths of Korean missionaries lie in evangelism and church planting, with a significant number also involved in theological training on the mission field. However, social action is recognised as an area of weakness among Korean missionary thinking (J. Ma 2011, 78–84; T. K. Park 2009, Loc. 1643).

God's Perfect Timing

The KMM emerged into the missionary world when traditional Western missions began experiencing declining numbers and activity. "The existence of the Korean missionary movement," says missiologist Warren Beattie, "challenges any perception that missionary sending is largely a thing of the past" (2017, 36). Professor of Global Christianity Wonsuk Ma, notes that the KMM's "growth and missionary development almost exactly coincides with the decisive turn in the shift of global Christianity" (W. Ma 2015, 371). Because of these facts, Korean Christianity has encouraged and influenced several Majority -World emerging missionary movements including Mongolia's. Interestingly, its growth also coincided with Korea's economic growth period suggesting that KMM's success is linked, at least partially, to socioeconomic development—a correlation that advocates further research and thought.

Precautionary Elements of the KMM

The KMM's zealous passion for evangelism and church planting cross-culturally has been a double-edged sword. According to J. Ma (2011, 81), this could reflect a possibly underdeveloped ecclesiology in the Korean church, one with a very strong local-congregational orientation as a monoculture. Consequently, a Korean missionary church plant can often be seen as a mirror or extension of their home church growth, creating a "Koreanising" of the planted church rather than an independently contextualised indigenous Church. This, J. Ma suggests, can become

> a visible sign of a [Korean] church's missionary accomplishment. Often church dedications become a celebration for the visitors from the sponsoring church, rather than for the congregation [indigenous church]. (81-82)

Homogenous societies like Korea (87) can also tend to analyse other cultures through their own cultural lenses and often struggle to adapt to new cultural situations. At this point it is important to note that this situation has been repeated throughout the history of Christianity by many missionary sending nations, such as Great Britain and America, and has been well-documented elsewhere.

While many deal with issues as they arise this should not replace the process of understanding the culture and allowing it to influence how I operate and how I view the Mongolians "because mission is always performed in the context of culture" (88). Monoculturalism can also result in people pushing their own values and practices onto host countries. Analysis of various church plants by Korean missionaries often reveals many Korean traits in Asian contexts including in Mongolia (J. Ma 2011, 90; T. K. Park 2009, loc. 1643).

Positive Elements

Positively, like the African movements the church in Korea exhibits a vibrant spirituality firmly outworked through a fervent praying church and movement, which many consider a fundamental element of its growth and sustainability (J. Ma 2011, 88). Like Mongolia, Korea's underlying worldview is shamanistic (89) which religious historian Amanda Porterfield defines as "a technique for attaining ecstasy that enables the persons to come into contact with the sacred order of the cosmos" (1987, 721). A danger of such spiritual awareness is that it can lead to syncretism with shamanistic practices (Kraft 2005, 9). Yet those with a spiritual reality to their everyday life experiences have the ability to explore and contextualise the spiritual nature of theology which is an essential element to self-theologising.

Western worldviews, on the other hand, influenced by the Enlightenment, have successfully removed the understanding of and belief in the everyday influence and place of supernatural forces in one's life creating what Hiebert describes as the "excluded middle" (1985, 189–201). This middle realm is where God is experienced and is directly involved in the human affairs of life (198). For Koreans and Mongolians who are at home in this middle world the challenge is to bring their cultural practices under the scrutiny of Scripture to avoid syncretistic practices in the churches. This is where what Hiebert calls "critical contextualisation" should be exercised (1994, chap. 4), a practice that will lead to self-theologising.

In summary, there are clear lessons to learn from the significant Korean Missionary Movement's impact on the Mongolian church. First, their zeal and commitment to the call of mission are amazing. Second, the strong relationship with the sending church and commitment to prayer for mission and missionaries are exemplary. But a cautionary note should be sounded concerning their monoculturalism. Like Korea, it could be a danger for Mongolia as Mongolians rediscover their national identity and cultural cohesiveness and the church reaches for its own identity. There is a potential danger of national pride in the process. Therefore, it is important that the Mongolian church develop a balanced theology and ecclesiology that are contextualised and Mongolian, while on the mission field they should be able to remain contextually flexible in missiological practice.

Singaporean Success

Another Asian neighbour with a strong missional church is Singapore. Like Korea, Singapore is a relatively young nation with a robust economy and a vibrant church. In 1970 the Christian population was estimated as just 2 percent of the population, whereas by 2010 it had grown to around 18 percent. Pastor and researcher Ivan Liew acknowledges that Singapore's strong economic growth and equally successful church growth give the church its strong missional element (2017, loc. 371). Like Korea, strong economic growth appears to be a key element in the equation of success.

In recent years extensive research conducted by Ivan Liew and others culminated in a missionary movement model he calls Church Missions & Agencies Together

(CMAT) (2017). The key concept in this model is to have a right relationship between the sending church and the sending agency, a partnership based upon four important factors,

1. The biblical centrality of the church in mission
2. The equal value of church and agency in mission
3. Glad submission and mutual deference between church and agency
4. Joyful fellowship and encouragement (loc. 912).

A partnership between the sending church and the sending agency anchored to these four elements creates the foundation for a potentially sustainable movement. Clearly defining the sending church's role and the mission agency's role and how they complement one another is the strength of this model. Within this framework, the three ingredients of a successful church agency partnership can be worked out: the vision of the movement, the ministry philosophy (operating procedures), and the financial elements (loc. 1285). This is a simple model yet effective. For a young missionary movement forming, like the one in Mongolia, this model has characteristics that Mongolians may want to adopt and adapt in their own movement.

Asian Missionary Movements (AMMs)

On a broader front, Filipino theologian David S. Lim in a blogpost, *Strategies of Mission Movements in Asia Today* (2013), highlights five main mission strategies that have been globally developed and applied by many AMMs on the mission field. These strategies he identifies and discusses under the following headings in the blogpost,

5. Church growth through outreach programs
6. Church growth through cell multiplication
7. Church growth through intentional church planting
8. Church multiplication through church planting movements

9. Kingdom expansion through disciple multiplication movements (2013).

Lim believes there is a need to prioritise the last two of these strategies in the twenty-first century. Every Christian, he argues, can and should be engaged in personal evangelism, even leading small groups at home or in the workplace, becoming lay leaders of informal churches in the process. But perhaps the fifth strategy, disciple multiplication movements (DMMs), is an even more effective strategy in creating people movements (2013).

Lim believes that much of traditional missionary effort today is still engaged in the first two or three methods and suggests that a paradigm shift towards DMMs is essential in the third millennium. It shifts away from professional/career missionaries and formally organised missions of Christendom and reintroduces the doctrine of the priesthood of all believers. Although the first three strategies will continue to be used to spread the gospel well into the future, they utilise only in part the whole body of the church to reach the unreached (2013). President of Gordon Conwell Theological Seminary, Scott Sunquist, also believes, "It is imperative that each local church find ways of releasing and empowering the laity to do the work of the mission of God" (2013, 309). It is good to remember that Jesus raised ordinary people to join his band of missionaries: fishermen, tax collectors, and zealots.

Summary

Each of these mission movement examples gives valuable insight into the requirements of forming a sustainable missionary movement. First, a balanced and contextualised theology and ecclesiology are essential for right missiological practice and the avoidance of potential syncretism. Second, there is the need for each of the different bodies involved in the missionary movement to have defined roles and to understand one another's roles and strengths within the whole movement, as shown in the Singapore model. And third, the move away from hierarchical structures and the professional or career missionaries towards seeing a return to empowering the laity within the church, gives hope to the Mongolian situation. The capacity to be involved in mission lies within everyone who believes. Finally, missionaries must always keep in mind that their goal is to share the gospel, not their interpretation nor simply to share their own culture. These are valuable elements of a cross-cultural missionary movement to help analyse the current Mongolian missionary movement.

Latin American Missionary Movements

The history of protestant evangelical mission to Latin America has been traced back to the Lutheran church first establishing a colony in Venezuela in 1528 (de Cavalho 2011, 57). However, Latin American missionary Decio de Cavalho, one of the founders of the Latin American missionary network, COMIBAM, writes that it was "not until the 1900s that the first denominational national mission entities were established and sent out missionaries" (59). Like Africa and several areas of Asia the situation reflects more than a century of colonial, imperialistic mission work in Latin America under different and various colonisers.

In 1910 the Latin Americans were excluded from the Edinburgh International Missionary Conference as certain persuasive parties convinced organisers that it was no longer a mission field. This disappointment of exclusion proved to be a God-given catalyst to heightened missionary activity and in 1916 a separate conference convened in Panama to discuss mission work across the continent (59). By the 1970s a number of mission entities had been established. In 1982 The Brazilian Mission Association was established as the first network to support the growing mission organisations within the Brazilian missionary movement. Other networks were to follow over the coming decades (60).

COMIBAM:

In 1987 the first Iberoamerican[3] mission congress took place in San Paulo, Brazil, with over 3000 representatives from across the continent. This meeting was the beginning of the now established COMIBAM. In 2017 the most recent congress in Bogota, Columbia, celebrated thirty years of mission from Latin America. According to historical documents, "COMIBAM is a network with an emphasis on mobilizing Latin Americans people in mission" and "sees the church as a missionary force, seeking to transform the Iberoamerican church as capable of extending the gospel to every nation" (Cueva 2016, 252–53). Despite the strong denominational and theological divides across the continent, it is an example of an extensive collaborative network that consists of three networks in partnership:

1. A pastors and leaders network;
2. A network of missionary training centres, interdenominational and denominational;
3. A network of sending structures to see missionaries sent out (257).

According to an article by Douglas Smith, entitled "COMIBAM Takeoff Towards AD 2007" (1998) COMIBAM's strengths focus primarily on intercessory prayer, cross-cultural training centres, and a focus on the unreached peoples of the world (Smith 1998). However, in *The Reshaping of Mission in Latin America* (2015), editor and missiologist Mireya Alvarez infers that its primary weakness is the variety of churches and denominations within Latin America, creating the need for dialogue between all parties concerning the mission movement within and from their continent (11–12).

---

[3] Iberoamerican refers those Spanish and Portuguese nations of the Americas

Integral Mission

Columbian theologian, J. Daniel Salinas, identifies three distinct approaches to mission by the Latin American church. First, there are those who do not directly participate in mission. It does not mean evangelism is absent, but simply that these churches lack the resources beyond their immediate environment to support missionaries in the traditional manner. Second are churches that send and support missionaries mainly through traditional foreign agencies working across Latin America. Latin Link International is an example of such an organisation.[4] According to Salinas, this second group of churches often lacks the structures in their nations to send missionaries and therefore partner with international missions. These churches learn to abide by these international agencies' traditional structures and requirements even though it brings financial burden to bear (2008, 141). The third group consists of those developing an indigenous Latin American theology of mission and evangelism (140-142). Out of this group has grown a contextualised evangelism relevant to the culture of Latin America: integral/holistic mission. Salinas suggests that Padilla defines integral mission as "the integration of two elements of the gospel that have been historically severed - social action and proclamation"(145).

Simply saving souls and planting churches (traditional mission), while centrally important to mission, is neither a complete nor a whole theology of mission according to Latin American missiologist and theologian Rene Padilla. Widely considered the father of integral mission, Padilla argues that integral/holistic mission is primarily concerned with crossing the frontier of faith and non-faith rather than geographical boundaries (2021, 22). At home or in foreign countries, the global church is responsible for fulfilling the *missio Dei* not just the chosen few cross-cultural missionaries. According to Salinas,

---

[4] Latin Link International's roots are British, although it has developed into an international community serving both missionaries to Latin America and from Latin America (Latin Link International 2015).

Padilla argued that an integral mission theology orientates towards satisfying all basic human needs; they include God, love, food, shelter, clothing, physical and mental health, and dignity (2008, 146). Although controversial in the late twentieth century, integral mission today is accepted and adopted worldwide especially within the Majority-World. While the Mongolian churches should not simply imitate Latin American integral/holistic mission, as they consider self-theologising they must ponder on what a holistic approach to mission means for Mongolia and its diaspora.

Brazilian theologian Valdir Steuernagal, in an article, "A Mission Voice From Latin America: Partnering for World Mission" (2008), sounds a note of caution concerning Latin Americans' passion for mission. He argues that it is important to learn from the past in humility. His four concerns are: (i) the church should not assume that because they are a Majority-World culture they understand the cultures of those to whom they are sent. Identification with other cultures on the mission field must not be assumed. (ii) Adequate and relevant training processes must be present, not just copying the myriad of programmes out there but designing and producing a relevant and applicable programme for the Latin American missionary in training. (iii) Perseverance on the field is critical to sustaining mission movements. While home cultures tend towards collective behaviour in some situations, missionaries must learn how to handle solitude and failure when they are outside their own cultures. (iv) Faithfulness in support is also important. Of this, he writes:

> In missionary terms, our history is one of dependence, and hence, reception. The fact that mission also implies giving is a concept which most of our churches are still learning. They must go through a complete learning process that will lead them to understand that missions is serious business, involving financial faithfulness to those we send out in Jesus' name. (Steuernagal 2008)

The Mongolian church will need to heed these comments, especially concerning the concept of mission as giving and then grasp the need for financial faithfulness in sending missionaries cross-culturally.

Summary

Each of the missiological histories provide through these three geographical regions highlights certain key areas of development for an emerging missionary movement. First is the need for a generation to emerge disentangled from historical and foreign influences unwittingly imparted by missionaries. Second is the need for adequate Bible knowledge and cross-cultural missionary training to be available to potential missionaries before departure. Third is the necessary involvement of the home church in financial commitment and support of their missionaries, all of which should be encompassed by a commitment to prayer. Fourth, partnerships, often necessary for Majority-World ventures, need to be carefully and prayerfully chosen for the mutual benefit of both parties and with a unified goal. Finally, it would be beneficial for Mongolians to understand their own cultural influences and characteristics as they embark on cross-cultural missionary life. As these are some of the essential elements necessary for a growing and vibrant missionary movement, it will be important to understand how the Mongolian cross-cultural missionary movement measures up against them. I will now turn attention in chapter 3 to exploring the Mongolian church and its cross-cultural missionary movement.

Chapter 3

Good Soil: A Mongolian Contextual Portrait

In this chapter, I intend to explore the emerging Mongolian missionary movement's cultural context by exploring the historical, religious, and political influences that have shaped today's church in Mongolia. However, due to the young nature of the evangelical church in Mongolia and its missionary movement, there is scant scholarly work available. A few biographical works and a few theses by Western and Korean missionaries are available concerning church growth in Mongolia. Despite this lack I hope that this chapter paints a picture of twenty-first century Mongolia's nature, culture, and status in order to frame the most relevant questions to explore and to understand what is required in developing a sustainable missionary movement.

To achieve this goal, this chapter will be divided into several sections: Mongolia's historical background, the religious and cultural basis of the people, followed by the contemporary political and economic situation into which the movement is currently being formed. Lastly, I will study the recent church history of Mongolia and the emerging missionary movement, bringing together both context and content so that the needs for ongoing research can be explored.

Historical Background

This section traces modern-day Mongolia from twelfth century nomadic tribes on the steppes of Asia to the present day showing the key influences that have shaped modern Mongolians.[1]

According to Mongolian historian Baabar, the origins of modern-day Mongolia lie in the twelfth century with the nomadic tribes of the steppes of inner Asia (1999, 21). Baabar observes that while these Mongol tribes loved their freedom, their warring ways ultimately shaped them into "a people who were unruly, proud and uninhibited with little sense of time" (7). This way of life meant that, potentially, the tribes of the steppe were destined for permanent obscurity. However, their outlook began to change towards the end of the twelfth century.

A young man called *Temuujin* (Тэмүүжин written in Mongolian) began uniting the scattered tribes of the steppe, eventually bringing them together as a united force under a single banner, establishing the Mongol empire in 1206. Around this time, Temuujin became better known as Genghis Khan (Чингис Хаан) translated as probably "Universal Ruler" (Bawden 2019). Before his death in 1227 Genghis Khan had successfully allied Europe and China with lasting diplomatic connections. Historian Jack Weatherford comments, "One of the enduring legacies of the Mongol empire was its facilitation of vigorous cultural exchange, knowledge, personnel, and technology between the East and the West" (2004, xix). Genghis Khan also established a rule of life for all his subjects throughout the empire, known as the *Yasa* (Kemp 2000, 76). As supreme ruler, he demanded full and undivided loyalty at all times. Genghis Khan himself practised shamanism and worshipped "the god of the Eternal blue sky," having the shamans

---

[1] The core text to which most writers of Mongolian history and culture reference is *The Secret History of the Mongols: The Life and Times of Chinggis Khan* (Onon 2005). Therefore, it is not surprising that it is a text from which several authors referenced below have sought clarification and validity.

perform rituals prior to any battle, readying the troops and literally inducing fear among the enemy ranks (Weatherford 2004, 47).

The expanding Mongol Empire, particularly under Kublai Khan (grandson of Genghis Khan), practised religious tolerance and included people of various religious persuasion, including Muslims and Christians, within the governing administration. It was not until the end of Kublai Khan's (Хубилай Хаан) reign in 1294 that Kublai began to favour Tibetan Lamaism (Kemp 2000, 116). Kemp points out that, as grandson to Genghis Khan, he was "the fifth and last of the great Khans, reigning from 1260 to 1294, for the first twenty years from Karakorum in the Mongol steppe heartland, then shifting his capital to Datu (Beijing) as first of the Yuan Emperors in China" (112).

Quite simply, Kublai became, like the apostle Paul, "all things to all men" (1 Cor. 9:22). As Weatherford notes, he won control of China by "appearing to be more Chinese than the Chinese" (2004, loc. 3668). In doing so Kublai conquered and unified all of China. By the end of his reign Kublai came to favour Buddhism, especially Tibetan Lamaism, which was as much a political move as a religious one. It meant that he did not have to conquer Tibet but simply acquired it through astute diplomacy (Kemp 2000, 116).

After Kublai Khan died turmoil again arose within the family as to who should be the successor, which Weatherford suggests bred fear within the royal family household (2004, loc. 4449). Worse still, outside the capital a far greater destroyer was being unleashed ultimately killing possibly as much as two-thirds of the population of China alone through its treachery (loc. 4471). Through the rest of the fourteenth century the Black Death, as it had become known, continued to destroy significant swaths of humanity across the world as it was spreading through the trade routes across the Empire and beyond.

As a result, deprived of their two advantages of military strength and commercial capital, it meant that each branch of the royal family across the Empire was left to search for fresh ways to maintain power and legitimacy (loc. 4554). In the South, Kublai's successors failed to grasp this notion and isolated themselves from those they ruled, aggravating the Chinese populous. By 1368, according to Weatherford, Mongol rule in China collapsed to the growing Ming rule under Emperor Taizu (loc. 4601).

In the mid-seventeenth century the Ming rulers, seeking help from a potential coup from within Beijing, sought aid from the Manchus in the north, who subsequently took advantage and seized power for themselves signalling the end of the Ming dynasty and the beginning of the Qing dynasty in 1644. This rule would last until early in the twentieth century (The Editors of Encyclopedia Britannica 2021). This autocratic rule would eventually bring pressure to bear on Mongolians in the north causing them to agree to come under the protection of the Manchu in order to survive.

However, the start of the twentieth century saw a significant wind of change blow into Mongolia as they were about to come out from under Qing rule and authority. On December 1, 1911, declares Mongolian historian Batsaikhan Ookhnoi, "the Mongols seceded from the Manchu Empire [Qing dynasty], declared their independence and elevated the Bogdo (Holy) *Jebtsundamba Khutuktu* to the throne as the Khan of the Mongolian nation" (Ookhnoi 2019, 1).[2] This is the beginning of change and preparation for future shifts that would take place within the religious landscape of Mongolia.

Buddhism had long since gained deep significance as a major part of Mongolian society not just as a religion but also in culture, economy, and even politics. Professor of Mongolian history Christopher Atwood notes that, in 1918, "census figures show that 105,577 men, or 44.6 percent, of the male population were registered as lamas" (2009,

---

[2] Bogdo (Holy) Jebtsundamba Khutuktu which translates as "the venerable incarnate lama". This is the eighth such reincarnated lama and as the eighth Jebtsundamba (1869–1924) was elevated to theocratic ruler and called the Bogd Khan. He was the head of state until his death in 1924.

325). Education, health care and many other spheres of society were under Buddhist influence. This environment would pose an issue for the Soviets, under which Mongolia would officially subsume its independence as the prototype of the satellite states of the USSR (1956, 39).[3] Over the next seventy years Soviet-induced systematic destruction of monasteries and temple artefacts began. During the late 1930s tens of thousands of Buddhist lamas were annihilated by the regime (Mongoliantemples 2014).

Mongolia would spend these years becoming increasingly closed to the outside world. During the same period the world would experience the formation of the Republic of China (1912), the Russian revolution (1917), two World Wars, and a dramatically changing global landscape. Mongolia simply slipped out of focus, nestling between two giant superpowers of the world (Sanders and Lattimore 2019).

In the late 1980s *Perestroika*[4] gripped the former Soviet Union radically restructuring the government in Russia. During this time Mongolia was energised to reforms and from within, movements towards true independence began gaining ascendancy. With the USSR on the verge of bankruptcy due primarily to satellite States like Mongolia, and the rise of independence movements in Mongolia, on March 9, 1990, the communist old guard stepped down from power and Mongolia finally gained full and true independence from Russian influence (Rossabi 2005, chap. 1).

Gaining independence from the influence of a crumbling Soviet Union, Mongolia established a multi-party system of governance with free elections and in 1992 a new constitution was ratified. For seventy years Mongolia had been closed to the outside world. During that period, almost six hundred years of Buddhism were systematically

---

[3] American orientalist, Owen Lattimore comments, "It is my contention that Outer Mongolia was first a satellite of Tsarist Russia from 1911 to the Russian Revolution and then became a satellite of Soviet Russia" (1956, 39), although the date of 1921 is the significant historical date marked for the Mongolian revolution, the details differ as to Russia's part in it depending on whose history one reads.

[4] Perestroika means restructuring or reform. It was Russian Presiedent Gorbachev's reform strategy for the former USSR.

dismantled by the Communist regime, creating a spiritual vacuum into which Christianity would flood.

Religion and Culture

Buddhism and Shamanism have significantly shaped modern Mongolia, giving them a strong sense of identity and belonging to Mongolia, the land and its culture. To better understand this trend, this section is divided into two: religious persuasions and cultural keys.

Religious Persuasions

As observed from the previous section, the predominant religion of Mongolia since the fourteenth century had been Mongolian Buddhism, a form of Tibetan Buddhism but with a unique Mongolian twist. As pastoral nomads, Mongolians traditionally value their connection with and reliance upon the natural elements and the spirit world which they believe hold sway over these elements. This animistic outlook and the shamanism through which it is practised plays a key role in shaping their culture and worldview. The morphing of Tibetan Buddhism with this underlying shamanistic worldview, the adopting of Buddhist deities, symbols and practices into their everyday lives, gave rise to the complex religious and cultural phenomenon called "Mongolian Buddhism" (Wallace 2015, xv). Marku Tsering succinctly describes it as "local gods appearing in Buddhist dress" (1993, 96). Not surprisingly, Mongolian Buddhism and Shamanism are considered the two primary religions of Mongolia today.

Tuvshintugs Dorj, a modern-day Mongolian shaman, has written insightfully in *Mongolians After Socialism* (2012), noting that shamanic traditions in Mongolia were not retained or properly written down during previous centuries and were virtually eradicated during the Soviet purges of the twentieth century. Many shamans during this period were rural dwellers and passed on their practices and beliefs through what Dorj calls "domestic teaching and transmission"—in other words, shamanistic practices were inherited rather than school taught (117). Hence, with Mongolia's newfound freedoms in the twenty-first century and through practitioners like Dorj, Shamanism is openly re-entering the lives and culture of Mongolians. Today, a reimaged shamanism is very much on the ascendency despite Christianity's presence. The shamanistic worldview of Mongolia (like many other Asian nations) permeates the very fibres of their being without even realising its presence. For the Mongolian, it is about living in harmony with nature and protecting the equilibrium of the environment through pleasing the spirits (119).

It is important also to mention the Muslim population of Mongolia. In the far west of Mongolia lies a region that borders China's Xinjiang province, Russia, and is close to Kazakhstan. Here Islam has a presence as Xinjiang Uighurs and Muslim Kazaks have traditionally interacted with Mongolians. While the 1992 constitution affords religious freedom in Mongolia, it officially recognises Buddhism, Shamanism, and Islam as the three named religions of Mongolia (The Constitutional Court of Mongolia 2017, Article 15:16).

Cultural Keys

Shamanistic cultures tend to live in a paradigm of fear versus power, power that is possessed by all the spirits that control their universe (Müller 2000, 42). However, according to the website Honorshame.com, Asian countries generally are predominantly honour/shame cultures with a partial mix of fear/power (Georges 2015a). The authors of the insightful honorshame.com website observe there is no one flavour of honour or shame; rather, different peoples have different ways of culturally expressing it (Georges 2015b). Jason Georges, the website's founder, in his book, *The 3D Gospel* (2014), describes honour/shame cultures as:

> Group personalities . . . . Just as individual people have a *person*-ality, cultural groups share a *group*-ality. Groupality refers to an "organized pattern of behavioural characteristics of a group. A person's cultural orientation, or groupality, shapes their worldview, ethics, identity, and notion of salvation, even more than their individual personality does. (loc. 129)

Whether to family, church, or village, belonging speaks to a person's worth, making group orientation important to a Mongolian. Consequently, as Georges notes, honour is bestowed when others think well of a person (Mongolian: someone is thought of as a good person). It brings harmony to the community. Likewise, shame is a negative rating in the community, resulting in disconnection from the group or community (Mongolian: someone thought of as a bad person). Therefore, a network of key relationships is vital in every aspect of life (loc. 231-234). This sense of belonging for the Mongolians will be significant from the perspective of forming a Mongolian missionary movement.

Mongolians also have a strong connection with the land itself. For example, one of Mongolia's poets likens the grasses under their feet to their ancestors. Literature professor Simon Wickham-Smith explains how these ancestors though not necessarily physically present are still literally and permanently connected with the land.

> Mongol nomadic life, of course, moves along a trajectory analogous with that of any other society, but the conception of this trajectory is defined by the relationship between the people moving across the land, the ancestors below the land and the sky god above. This shamanic model has been . . . somewhat syncretised with Buddhist thought, but it still holds sway throughout Mongolia's cultural life. (2019, 6)

Showing the importance of Genghis Khan in a Mongolian's life, Wickham-Smith notes that Genghis flows like a "golden thread" linking the past, present and future together in modern Mongolian society. This thinking "creates of Mongolia a highly secure and homogenous society, one in which the importance of tradition and of the family of Mongolia is central" (8).

Even though Mongolian culture today is being challenged and influenced by globalisation and urbanisation, these underlying tendencies of groupality and their sense of space and time remain firm. Therefore, it is important for the Mongolian church and cross-cultural missionary movement to understand these deeper worldview influences. Though much of the surface culture is shifting, these core elements make Mongolians who they are in the world and before God.

It is evident from the above characteristics that the cross-cultural missionary movement will need to provide a strong sense of belonging. This sense of belonging may come through strong relationships or partnerships with others sharing their goals and ideals. Perhaps it will come through their unified sense of calling to the wider Mongol diaspora as a golden thread running through their movement alongside that of Genghis Khan, as, in one way, it is in his footsteps and through his grass they tread.

In summary, religion and culture play a significant role in shaping twenty-first century Mongolians. They are deeply spiritual beings, even those who claim they have no religion, as observed by their love of the land. Christianity currently stands at 1 percent of the population while Buddhism stands at 51.7 percent (United States Government, Central Intelligence Agency 2022). However, how much Mongolian Christians are conscious of their own cultural influences or can understand how it shapes them remains to be seen.[5]

Contemporary Political and Economic Status

As a modern democratic society, Mongolia is young and inexperienced. It is a nation still forming its national identity and its political and economic stability. This section explores how this impacts the church and its future.

---

[5] *Mongolian Proverbs* by Janice Raymond, (2014) is a significant book for understanding this aspect of Mongolian life; Mongolian proverbs reflect their understanding and begin to reveal their deep-seated cultural identity.

Since Mongolia's independence in 1990 urbanisation has played a significant role in transforming the country's economy. Several severe winters in recent times have seen many rural herders converge onto the capital city or provincial (*aimag*) centres to seek more financially stable lifestyles. In the last twenty-five years the capital city (Ulaanbaatar) alone has seen its population rise from around 660,000 in the 1990s to approximately 1,400,000 in 2015; roughly half the population (World Population Review 2022). Today, discoveries of mineral deposits are transforming Mongolia into a mineral-rich nation. Consequently, over the last twenty years the mining sector has played a significant part in the economic growth and focus of the country (Baatarzorig, Galindev, and Maisonnave 2018, 527).

Nevertheless, several vulnerabilities threaten the fragile Mongolian economy. First, as a landlocked nation it is dependent on the economic needs of its two main neighbours: Russia and China. Fluctuations in commodity prices such as coal and copper have proven in the recent past to have destabilising effects on Mongolia's economy, as experienced in the dip in prices in the mid-2000s (Batdelger et al. 2018). Mongolia lacks the experience and expertise to strengthen the mining sector, not to mention the required financial resources. Therefore, it relies heavily upon the larger international conglomerates to invest.

Additionally, as a fragile and inexperienced democracy it makes frequent changes to the law which cause further instability. This practice makes the necessary international investors nervous (Blaauw 2013). Corruption at governmental levels is perhaps the greatest vulnerability to economic stability. According to the corruption rankings on the Trading Economics website, Mongolia ranked ninety-three out of 175 in 2018. In 2020 it ranked 111th (Trading Economics 2020). Naturally these economic uncertainties have an indirect bearing on the financial well-being of the church as misappropriation of limited funds is not just confined to governments. With mission thinking still in the development stage of this first-generation church, as suggested in chapter 1, it can become easy for churches to alter priorities on funding. Often, monies given for mission appear to be appropriated to other causes.

The Mongolian Church: First-Generation Implications

Waiting and praying in countries across Eastern Europe during the late 1980s were numerous missionary groups. Sensing the imminent collapse of the Soviet Union, they were preparing to enter Mongolia. When the country opened in 1991 they entered, discovering there were only a handful of existing believers (Visser, Byambatseren, and Stephens 2019, 7; Austin 2017, 64). Seventy years of socialism had effectively broken the backbone of Buddhist dominance of the previous centuries leaving a spiritual vacuum into which these missionaries brought the love of Jesus. According to historian Morris Rossabi, they were among the first philanthropic aid organisations to pour into Mongolia (2005, 40).

Today, there are various missionary accounts of what happened as Christianity swept across the country in those early years (Hogan 2008; Leatherwood 2006). Over the last couple of decades, articles and blog posts containing diverse stories and estimates have been written about how fast the church grew and how numerous it might be today. Sadly, many of them are inaccurate (Advancing Native Missions 2016; Roberts 2011). These simply indicate how little actual research has been undertaken and how hard it is to accomplish such research in Mongolia.

According to surveys in 2020 by the Mongolian Evangelical Alliance (MEA), there are approximately thirty-three thousand believers in the churches across Mongolia today, around one percent of the population (Mongolian Evangelical Alliance 2020;

Visser, Byambatseren, and Stephens 2019).[6] These figures clearly vary from previous, enthusiastic estimates. One of the difficulties is who to count. Second, when asked for numbers pastors will automatically give an inflated reading to be seen in a favourable light. The 2019 survey utilised a questionnaire given specifically to individual members within congregations to avoid some of these issues (2019). Most of the other figures in the various accounts of what happened were generally collated from what was perceived rather than through any formal research, and as previously noted, in their enthusiasm the Mongolians have a cultural propensity to elevate the numbers.

The Journey of Christianity in Mongolia

Prior to 1991 the earliest record of Christian presence within Mongolia is with Nestorian Christians in the seventh century, according to missiologist Hugh Kemp's work *Steppe by Step* (2000). In the fifth century Nestorius was briefly Bishop of Constantinople before being accused and condemned of heresy resulting in exile from the church. Kemp notes that this incident would have ramifications for Christianity in Mongolia 1600 years later (25).

As a result of this banishment Nestorius headed East from his homeland, joining the Eastern church in Persia. His followers became closely linked with the trade success of Mesopotamia. By the eighth century he had made Bagdad the Nestorian capital of the world (33) and a strategic location on the Silk Road. Nestorians became involved in trading out of Bagdad along the route East which would take them into China and parts of Mongolia. Kemp notes that they established centres in key towns, which would become places of learning and eventually some of the first-ever missionary training schools (33-34).

---

[6] These figures represent the number of believers attending church as opposed to those simply attending church who are perhaps not yet belivers. According to the MEA report in 2020 there were approximately 46,350 attendees and 33,000 believers (Mongolian Evangelical Alliance 2020, 18).

The next event to have a significant bearing on Christianity in Mongolia was during the reign of Kublai Khan (1260-1294). According to the publication *World Christian Trends, AD 30-AD 2200* (2001), in 1260 Kublai reportedly made a request through Marco Polo to the church in Rome asking for

> 100 men skilled in your religion . . . . If they were convincing . . . I shall be baptized, and then all my barons and great men, and then their subjects. And so there will be more Christians here than there are in your parts. (Barrett et al. 2001, 124)

This request was never taken seriously and only a handful of priests were sent, none of whom arrived in Kublai's court. By the end of the century Tibetan Buddhism had become the favoured religion. This scenario, suggests the publication's editors, was the greatest missed opportunity in Christian history (124). Apart from a few missionary forays in the eighteenth and nineteenth centuries Christianity appeared to make very little inroads into Mongolia, Nestorianism vanished, and Buddhism ruled until the end of the nineteenth century.

Perhaps the most notable of these missionaries, from a British perspective, was James Gilmour of the London Missionary Society who set sail for Mongolia in 1870. He carried his possessions in a rucksack on his back and was soon considered akin to the wandering lamas of the day. However, it was his use of medicine that opened doors of opportunity for him to share the good news. Although, towards the end of his life he acknowledged seeing very little lasting fruit from his labours. James Gilmour died in 1891 of typhoid fever (Lovett 1908, 302). Thus, as the nineteenth century concluded and the twentieth century loomed bright Mongolia would break from under one giant's control (China) only to be subsumed under another (USSR).

In summary, historians note that from the early time of the Nestorians until 1991 there has never been an indigenous church within what is modern-day Mongolia. Throughout history the country remained predominantly Buddhist and, deeper still, shamanistic in outlook. However, in 1991 with only a few believers the church grew by a sovereign move of God. Initially the lack of indigenous traditions allowed the church to grow exponentially (Hattaway 2004, 20).

Authentic indigenous churches require authentic indigenous ecclesiology. While some Mongolian believers have been educated to a postgraduate level, it is largely through Western or Asian accredited theological programmes using traditional Western curricula. As noted earlier, Hiebert considers that it takes three to four generations before true indigenous theologising can happen (1985, 196). As the church in Mongolia moves into its second generation it is transitioning, searching for true identity and debating how to apply biblical theology in Mongolia. Second, there is a lack of mature leadership due to the young nature of the church (A. Hays 2017). While some have served in leadership capacities for more than twenty-five years, the ability of the younger leaders to deal with many of the scenarios of life that are often presented to them is limited, which often necessitates leaning on outside counsel. How that counsel is given and by whom is extremely important.

The Mongolian Cross-Cultural Missionary Movement

In 2019 a presentation in Mongolia of some unpublished research[7] on the care of Mongolian missionaries identified approximately sixty known Mongolians serving as long term cross-cultural missionaries (J. Park 2019, 31). Most of these are in some measure directly connected with international mission organisations in their chosen locations, principally among the Mongol diaspora across Asia. However, researchers Visser, Bayambatseren and missiologist Kwai Lin suggest that only 23 percent of churches have sent out missionaries beyond Mongolia's borders. Yet, a total of 45

---

[7] The research was a Capstone Project offered by Korean missionary to Mongolia in partial fulfilment of an "MA in Whole Person Health & Development" 2019 for "University of the Nations" Kona, Hawaii.

percent of churches are involved in church planting to some degree within their immediate community (42).

Several Mongolian sending organisations have emerged during the last decade, most linked with already established international organisations. One example is the Mongolian Mission Centre (MMC), primarily a YWAM base founded in Erdenet by Swedish YWAM missionaries in the 1990s. Currently, YWAM has bases in four cities in Mongolia. These bases offer a range of training found in any other YWAM base worldwide.[8]

Another of these organisations is Diaspora Mongolia Network (DMN) initially linked to a South Korean organisation of the same name. As an organisation it primarily reaches Mongolians who are in countries immediately bordering Mongolia or are Mongolian migrant workers abroad; in 2007 there were approximately 30,000 in South Korea alone (Wan and Pocock 2009, loc. 5256). According to the United Nations, in 2017 there were estimated to be 130,000 migrant Mongolian workers across the world (International Organization for Migration 2018). However, it is fair to say that economic factors since 2019 and the COVID 19 pandemic have caused this number to fluctuate significantly.

Most of these organisations produce difficult-to-find literature or statistics concerning the building blocks of their organisation and progress to date, and few are actually registered with the Mongolian government. Instead, those involved with larger international organisations like Campus Crusade (Cru) or Youth With A Mission (YWAM)[9] simply utilise their partners' websites and general documentation. However, these data are often only available in English or Korean making it hard for Mongolians to access this material. Finally, some missionaries are known to be sent directly by their

---

[8] These trainings include, Discipleship Training School (DTS) and the School of Biblical Studies (SBS) and School of Family Studies (SFS) https://ywam.org/location/ywam-ulaanbaatar-mongolia/b-661/

[9] www.cru.org; www.ywam.org

church which may be sufficiently large enough and well-funded from outside sources; therefore, they do not understand the need or place of Mongolian missionary sending agencies.

Much needs to be achieved in assessing the current number of missionary organisations and their status if the Mongolian church is to understand, consolidate and strengthen the current condition of its mobilisation efforts. The country is still young and attempting to reimage a new identity for itself as is the Mongolian church. Just as the nation has looked to the larger international corporations and banks to aid in its growth, the church and its missionary movement currently look to experienced international organisations for structure and financial support.

Summary

These three chapters spanning the literature review have covered extensive ground. Chapter 1 began with exploring and identifying a proper biblical perspective of mission as first, the mission of God (*missio Dei*), and second, acknowledges the church's primary role in fulfilling this mission under the authority of Jesus Christ (John 20:21) and in the power of the Holy Spirit (Acts 1:8). I then considered social movements and their organisational elements. It is important to have the right people involved, especially in leadership, those with vision and purpose who can understand and articulate the movement's goals. I considered the need for partnerships and networks in the case of the Mongolian cross-cultural missionary movement, which is young and small, including what these partnerships might look like and with whom should they partner.

In chapter 2 I explored examples of missionary movements from the Majority-World, highlighting how a nation's history and external cultural influences affect its worldview and, consequently, its church. These examples show the importance of the Mongolian church identifying a Mongolian contextual theology and ecclesiology leading to right missiology. The process of self-theologising was observed as a key to indigenising movements but something which can take until the third or fourth generation to formulate according to Hiebert (1985, 196). I considered how this will affect the process of building a strong missionary movement in Mongolia. Another key element to this building process is the importance of partnerships in a young movement like the Mongolian cross-cultural missionary movement, studying how these partnerships might take shape and with whom.

Finally, in chapter 3 I explored the contextual background of the current Mongolian church and its cross-cultural missionary movement and discovered a nation and church still in the process of building a solid identity. I observed several residule elements within society from the communist era, leaving it distrustful and cautious in building relationships. Yet, the Mongolian church is a first-generation church with a passion and a zeal to see the gospel message reach out among the Mongol diaspora.

The most significant gap to emerge from the literature was the lack of available material on the Mongolian church and its cross-cultural missionary movement. As a first-generation church and movement, this is not surprising. However, this lack of research necessitates that the first part of this study should be to evaluate the current Mongolian missionary movement and assess its strengths and weaknesses. Such research and evaluation was the purpose of this dissertation, and the design and results of that research are covered in part II.

Part II

Understanding the Here and Now While Looking to the Potential of the Future

Part I considered the available precedent literature to understand the necessary elements of successful missionary movements and attempts to paint a contextual portrait of the Mongolian church. In part II, I will explain the methods employed to analyse the Mongolian cross-cultural missionary movement's structure and well-being, seeking to assess the movement's strengths and weaknesses in light of the literature review to consider a way forward.

Chapter 4

Methodology for Gathering the Data

In the previous chapters, I identified the need to establish a clearer understanding of the Mongolian cross-cultural missionary movement and its current status before considering ways of strengthening and sustaining it for the future. In chapter 4 I will describe the methodology employed to accomplish this task. I begin with a brief note of the challenges of undertaking this research during the COVID pandemic and the security concerns faced. Next follows a rationale for the study before looking at the chosen research samples and the challenges of accessing them. I continue with a summary of the methods used to collect the necessary data and the limitations experienced in that process. Finally, I consider the reliability and validity of the study in these circumstances.

Research Challenges: COVID-19 and Security Issues

At the time of convening this study, in the fall of 2018, no one could have foreseen the COVID pandemic that was about to unfold upon an unsuspecting world nor the devastating effects it would have upon people movement or human life. As a result of the pandemic, by the end of January 2020 most nations began to restrict internal movement and close borders, restricting international travel. Unfortunately, due to its proximity and significant border with China, Mongolia was no exception, swiftly enacting lockdowns and imposing strict restrictions on face-to-face meetings. Due to these factors Mongolia was probably more tightly locked down than many other nations.

As a consequence of the pandemic the research phase of this project had to be adjusted to meet new schedules and requirements. Nevertheless, the majority of the intended interviews were conducted in Chiang Mai, Thailand, just days before countries began their lockdown procedures. Due to the restrictions after January 2020, completing focus groups and the remaining interviews in Mongolia would take many more months.

The second significant influence that shaped this research and the availability of sample populations was security issues. At the beginning of the research process, pre-COVID, most of the cross-cultural missionaries were ministering among minority Mongol peoples located in cities across China or in other nations, sensitive to the work of Christian missions. Due to the sensitive nature of their location and limited communication resulting from these security issues, the number of cross-cultural missionaries available for interview was also limited.

The COVID pandemic eventually displaced many of the Mongolian cross-cultural missionaries with most returning to Mongolia after some time. However, the necessary government restrictions to combat the spread of the virus meant meeting for interviews or focus groups was still not possible but had to be delayed, as will be explained further on. Nevertheless, I believe sufficient interviews were accomplished to provide the necessary data for this study to proceed. Eventually, as this chapter will indicate, two focus groups were able to be completed.

Research Rationale and Choice of Methods

This section explains the rationale behind this research project. I begin by sharing some personal background as to my competence and standing to undertake this research and will briefly share my observations that led to this research. Next, I will address the gaps in knowledge concerning the Mongolian cross-cultural missions that were exposed by the literature review that this research aims to fill by using appropriate research methodology for the Mongolian context.

Personal Background

I have worked among the Mongolian people in Mongolia since early 1993. I have had the privilege of seeing a first-generation church grow from literally a handful of seeds to the harvest and mission movement we see and experience today; that of a maturing plant of roughly 35,000 members throughout the country (Mongolian Evangelical Alliance 2020, 18). In the last decade, a growing passion has arisen within the Mongolian church to see the gospel taken out from Mongolia, across borders into the wider world, especially among the Mongolian diaspora, throughout the surrounding nations and across Central Asia, in fact, anywhere the Mongol Empire once controlled. For a modern-day glance of the Mongol Empire overlayed on the world, see map 1 below.

In light of the strong influences of missionaries to Mongolia and foreign pressures upon the church growth in the country, I am concerned with the kind of missionary movement that is emerging and whether those same influences are shaping the cross-cultural missionary movement. From observations and the literature review thus far, initial evidence suggests these elements are prevalent. The same evidence suggests the current movement is not sustainable in the long term (e.g., local funding, denomination competition, leadership issues, etc.) Therefore, this situation prompted my research in the hope of moving towards finding a solution for the long term. My longevity of service in Mongolia gives me a privileged position of trust to conduct this research and analyse the current cross-cultural missionary movement.

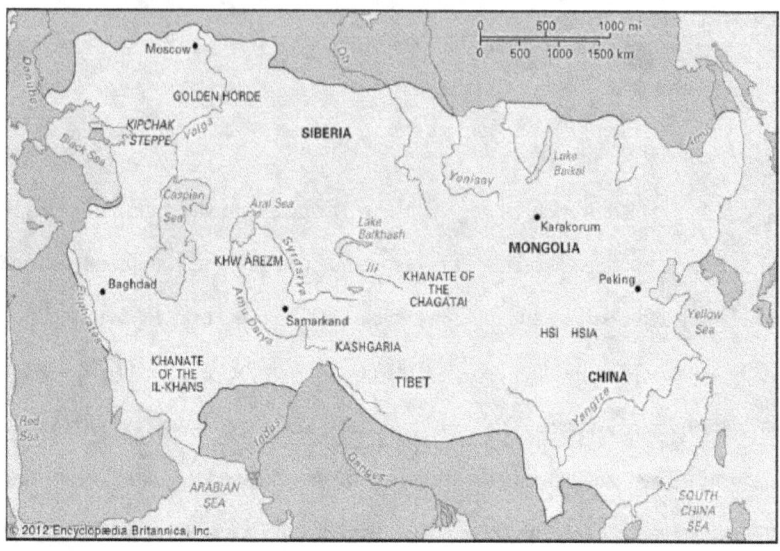

Map 1: The Former Mongol Empire in Today's World
(Encyclopedia Britannica 2020)

The Issue Being Addressed

Part I explored and identified from the literature review core elements that comprise a healthy and sustainable Majority-World missionary movement, elements that could act as a catalyst to encouraging and developing a sustainable cross-cultural missionary movement in Mongolia. Howard Brant's seven essentials (2009) for such movements, discussed at the end of chapter 1, offers a matrix through which to filter the data in chapter 5 and to build a coherent picture of what is and what needs to be.

Chapter 3 specifically considered the contextual background of the Mongolian cross-cultural missionary movement. In the process, it was clear that due to this being a first-generation church and subsequent missionary movement there is a lack of information and insufficient scholarly works available to gain a completely accurate picture of the Mongolian cross-cultural missionary movement. This lack of literature suggests that the first necessary outcome of this project is to accurately assess the Mongolian cross-cultural missionary movement through the current participants' eyes and understanding.

The second outcome is to tailor the research to indicate the presence or not of the core elements identified in the literature review for a healthy and sustainable movement. These will be achieved through the following field research questions which form the foundation of the questions in the interview guides for each sample group (see appendix A, B, C).

1. What are some key elements of a successful and sustainable cross-cultural missionary movement?
2. What are some of the challenges Mongolian missionaries face when ministering in a cross-cultural environment?
3. Can you identify, from your experience, some of the strengths and weaknesses of the current Mongolian missionary movement?
4. How do you understand the relationship between the missionaries, sending churches and the sending organisations involved in this missionary movement?

The Research Sample

This research project was conducted among Mongolians directly involved with the Mongolian cross-cultural missionary movement, thus, all participants are Mongolian. Consequently, I conducted all research in the Mongolian language.

As a country, Mongolia is roughly the size of Western and Central Europe combined, with a small population of just over 3,300,000 people (Sanders, Harris, and Lattimore 2021). One report suggests the Mongolian church is a little over one percent of the people and the cross-cultural missionary movement represents a proportion of that one percent (Visser, Byambatseren, and Stephens 2019). According to an official

Mongolian census of 2020, 59.4 percent of the population over the age of fifteen considered themselves religious, of whom 87.1 percent declared themselves Buddhists. Shamans, Christians, Muslims; others constitute the remaining 16.9 percent with Christianity representing 2.2 percent (National Statistics Office of Mongolia 2021, 61).

With the lack of clear data it is also difficult to establish exact numbers of Mongolian cross-cultural missionaries serving in other countries. According to research undertaken by JungMi Park (2019), a Korean Missionary to Mongolia, there were approximately sixty in 2018. However, during the interview stage of this research project, one of the participants put this figure at fifty,[1] and we know that due to the consequences of COVID that number has diminished further. Therefore, finding the necessary significant number of participants was challenging to ensure a viable and reliable research study. Nevertheless, utilising connections and relationships developed over the past twenty or more years of service in Mongolia, I am confident that those selected for this study are a fair and significant representation of the cross-cultural missionary movement.

Size of Sample Populations

I selected three target groups of people from which to draw participants. These three represent the main constituents of the cross-cultural missionary movement. They are: (1) the cross-cultural missionaries, (2) the leadership of churches that have sent cross-cultural missionaries, and (3) the leadership of the Mongolian missionary sending agencies.

- From group one: fifteen participants, including five couples and five singles
- From group two: seven participants

---

[1] This was given by one of the interviewees (SA6). It is also based upon extracting the number of those who are known to have returned from field service since the survey was completed.

- From group three: six participants

This gave me twenty-eight participants at this initial stage of research. Finally, the age range of the participants is between twenty-five and fifty-five (see appendix D). For the two focus groups completed most participants were among those twenty-eight.

While it was difficult to determine the exact numbers of representatives within each population group, as noted above, I am confident that each sample contains a fair representation and realistic percentage of their particular population. However, not being able to calculate the total numbers available within each population with any certainty, I have not attempted to give a percentage that would represent such a total.

Representation of Sample Populations

It should be noted that all of the missionary participants have a measure of connection to Pioneers[2] as an international missionary sending organisation. Of course, not all participants would consider themselves members of Pioneers, but whether through field team relationships or in a more formal manner, all the missionaries interviewed have a direct or indirect relationship with Pioneers due to Pioneers being one of the first missions working in Mongolia to offer its network of teams on the field and develop the opportunity for the Mongolian missionaries to serve.

Second, it was problematic to establish how many independent missionary sending agencies exist in Mongolia instead of churches that directly connect with agencies to raise support and opportunity for their missionaries. Of the sending agencies chosen it is worth noting that most only represent one or two missionary families at the time of this project. However, all are directly involved with the cross-cultural missionaries chosen to interview. Where possible, I selected a balance of experience, age

---

[2] www.pioneers.org. The researcher is a member of Pioneers while on the field of service but in the UK is a member of UFM Worldwide. These two organisations have a partnership agreement.

and length of service among the participants in order to gain a reasonable cross-section and fair representation of the movement. Therefore, I trust that, as anthropologist H. Russell Bernard points out, each was carefully and deliberately selected for a specific purpose rather than randomly (2006, 189).

Accessing the Research Population

Due to the sensitive nature of Christianity in the countries where many of the cross-cultural missionaries were ministering, some Human Subject Research (HSR) concerns affected the choice and availability of the participants. Mitigating these circumstances proved challenging as security experts considered even encrypted video calls pose a potential risk for those in these high-security conscious countries. However, all of the cross-cultural missionaries had some form of connection to Pioneers. God's timing is always perfect, for Pioneers had wanted, for a while, to facilitate the Mongolian missionaries to undergo security training required for all their missionaries ministering in areas of risk. This security training was finally arranged and held in in early January 2020[3] in Chiang Mai, Thailand, a country not deemed a security risk.

All of the missionary participants in this research were invited to attend except for one couple. I was able also to attend and, with the permission of Pioneers, scheduled interview times with each of the missionaries. Thus, reducing the security risk factor in this instance. Lastly, to safeguard each participant's identity, they are only referred to by a code throughout the analysis (appendix D). As there are no security issues surrounding the freedom of religion in Mongolia, the other two sample groups were freely available for interview within Mongolia.

---

[3] As this research raised some security concerns for both the researcher and the participants, the research design was vetted and approved by Fuller Seminary's Committee on Human Subject Research for conformance to ethical guidelines for the protection of research participants (approval received by email from the committee on the 17/12/2019).

Protocol for the Research Process

At the beginning of each interview and focus group, I clearly defined the project and answered any concerns or questions at that point. Once I was comfortable that each participant understood, I presented them with an appropriate informed consent form in Mongolian (appendix E) outlining the project and their rights as participants. This same form also clearly delineated the purpose and goal of the project. Each was encouraged to sign only upon reading and agreeing to all three pages. Surprisingly, most participants happily read the document before signing, which is not necessarily a given in these circumstances as a relationship of trust and respect can often override the need to read such documents carefully.

Methods: The Tools Used to Gather the Information

This project employed two data collection methods. The primary method was semi-structured interviews with open-ended questions conducted with each participant. While the questions roughly took the same route through the research topic, each population group had a slightly different approach to the question structure. This difference in question structure was in order to apply the research to their particular role as either a missionary, sending church representative or agency representative to attempt to understand the movement from their different perspectives (see appendices A, B, C).

Second, I conducted two focus groups to further explore some of the data findings. Unfortunately, due to the subsequent lockdown protocols in many places including Mongolia, it was necessary to postpone these groups until September 2020. Due to the time factor on this project there was insufficient time to undertake more than these two focus groups, but the focus group input was quite valuable.

While this initially left me with only one primary research method with which to begin the analysis, I knew that the three distinct populations came with equally distinct perspectives that could hold each other accountable in the absence of mixed methods. Supporting this approach, missiological researcher Edgar Elliston suggests that with missiological research there is a need to choose one primary method and supplement it with other materials such as field notes and observations (2011, loc. 3314). In *Analyzing Qualitative Data* (2007), Professor Graham Gibbs introduces the idea of constant comparisons as a technique to use during the coding stage as a way of checking constants as researchers go through the process of data analysis. He suggests there are two aspects to this process, (1) use the comparisons to check the "consistency and accuracy of application of codes"; and (2) "look explicitly for differences and variations in the activities, experiences, actions," etc., of the respondents interviewed (96). The following section considers the data collection methods in more detail.

Data Collection

This section will first explain the semi-strucutred interview process used for data collection and consider some of their strengths and weaknesses. Following this, I will explain the challenge of the focus groups and beofre considering their strengths and weakness.

Semi-Structured Interviews

As noted above, I chose semi-structured interviews with open-ended questions as my primary method of gathering data, as Elliston recommends (2011, loc. 3314). Bernard also suggests this method is best when there is possibly only one opportunity of interviewing the subject (2006, 212). Under the Mongolian Health Ministry's restrictions at the time, and with the cross-cultural missionaries' security concerns, this was precisely the scenario I faced.

Semi-structured interviews also present a broad scope of opportunity while addressing specific topics (Galletta and Cross 2013, 25). These interviews were structured only in the sense that I followed a predetermined set of questions (see appendices A, B & C) and I had prepared an extra list of probing questions for use when and where necessary to keep the conversation flowing and focused. How the questions are styled was influenced by an appreciative enquiry (AI) approach (Hammond 1998). The focus throughout the interview process was to identify the positive elements of the participant's experience within the missionary movement and to consider the weaknesses revealed in the light of the positives. While the questions were styled with an AI approach, analysis was styled by grounded theory which uses the constant comparison of data and formulates theories from the data as the process continues and can suggest new directions of inquiry (Charmaz 2014, 1).

Consequently, the interview questions were open-ended in nature allowing for a more free-flowing narrative while remaining on topic. The desired length of each interview was approximately one hour to one and a half hours maximum. In reality, they varied from between twenty-five and seventy-five minutes, reflecting respondents' individual personalities (some were more talkative than others). All interviews were conducted solely in Mongolian. Once all interviews were complete, the recordings were transcribed into Mongolian before being translated into English for analysis. The entire transcribing/translating task was conducted by a good friend fluent in both English and Mongolian and involved in a Bible translation project. Finally, I personally undertook to back-translate each interview as I received them using the audio recordings and the written Mongolian documents.

There are several notable strengths when using semi-structured interviews. The face-to-face value of the conversation allows researchers to observe the narrative and the body language, the slight inflexions of the eyes, the folding of the arms, or the raising of the voice in response to certain questions. They allow the opportunity to offer clarity when the question is unclear for the participant and the opportunity for the researchers to probe further when needed (Bernard 2006, 256). For interviews to be effective, the setting and environment for the interviews are equally important (Leedy and Ormrod 2010, 149). This process of considering the environment was beneficial as, in a few cases, the researcher and the interviewee did not have a previous relationship.

Second, having the set question format allowed me to obtain consistent and comparable data across all the interviews. The open-ended nature of the questions and resultant free-flowing dialogue provided sufficient content to extrapolate valuable and reliable data. Third, Bernard notes that it is recognised today that conversational style interviews, such as semi-structured interviews, can produce more accurate data than was previously thought possible (2006, 256).

A potential weakness of an interview was the need to possibly interview over distance, especially involving any potential follow-up interviews. While theoretically and technologically possible, it would have been more difficult in the time frame allotted at this stage. Fortunately, this only occurred once, causing me to interview one sending agency director (SA4) via Skype. It is worth noting that there was a marked difference in the quality of the interview conversation which was much more stilted or formal. It proved challenging to gain free-flowing dialogue even though the participant is well acquainted with the researcher the topic. Not being face to face physically, in a neutral environment but in our own settings, leant itself to distractions. It seemed as though the physical distance was tangible.

Another potential weakness with more narrative, free-flowing style interviews is that the interviewee, out of respect and honour for the interviewer, can potentially present inaccurate information, offering the interviewer what is perceived as the right answer to gain favour. I attempted to mitigate this potential weakness by carefully crafting the questions and having them translated into Mongolian by a Mongolian Bible translation project manager with a doctorate from Cambridge UK, whose command of English is impeccable. Therefore, I was confident that he had accurately translated the questions, and I was aware that this gentleman would have flagged any possible problems with inaccurate responses.

In addition to these precautions, as mentioned earlier, the relationships I have cultivated over the past decades ensured a measure of trust and respect and also meant I could recognise when respondents were holding back. In this case, I utilised some of the prepared prompts.

Focus Groups

I had planned focus groups to discuss some of the challenges within the movement that arose from the data. Thankfully, despite the COVID pandemic, two of these groups were undertaken late in the research period. While more were intended, these two were nonetheless valuable. One of the pandemics pluses was that many of the Mongolian cross-cultural missionaries eventually found themselves back in Mongolia, unable to travel out of the country. This made them more readily available to participate in focus groups. The idea was for each group to catalyse discussion on a particular issue that arose from the interviews and consider the way forward or any plausible solutions to the problem. These two groups consisted of six individuals for focus group one, and although five participants were due to take part in focus group two (appendix D), for personal reasons only three participated, but it was still profitable.

I facilitated these two groups myself, and an assistant kept a record of who spoke and the order in which they spoke. The two groups followed the same procedures concerning protocol and agreement as in the interviews, with first-time participants signing consent forms. Like all participants of this research, those involved with these two groups were coded accordingly to preserve individual confidentiality of responses. There was an advantage to these groups taking place during the later phase of the research as it gave me more time to prepare the questions once I had analysed the initial data.

One of the strengths of these groups was the ability to take a reoccurring topic from the interviews and allow the group to discuss the issue openly and generate possible solutions. It gave insight into the various characters and attitudes of the different participants concerning a challenging topic (Litosseliti 2003, 18). While no definitive answers were forthcoming or necessarily expected, these groups generated interest in talking further and planned how to do so. The two chosen topics under discussion were children's education on the mission field and sustainable finances within the movement, both potential barriers to growing and sustaining this cross-cultural missionary movement.

Some of the disadvantages of focus groups can be the presence of a dominant voice of those passionate about certain topics (Leedy and Ormrod 2010, 157) or the tendency to defer to certain leaders or those with experience in the particular area under discussion. Simple rules of engagement mitigated these issues, made easier by the need for participants to speak one at a time because of the recording and translation process. Furthermore, as the group facilitator and having a good relationship with each participant, I made sure each voice was heard equally, especially being sensitive to the quieter ones.

Pre Testing

The interviews were pre-tested prior to the main research beginning enabling me to adjust and refine the questions and the interview process. The pre-test was run twice, once with a former missionary awaiting the opportunity to return to a challenging location and then with an administrative assistant of one of the sending churches, who has a reasonable command of English. The pre-tests were both useful in helping me hone the questions. In addition, both pre-tests gave me valuable insight into timings and understanding of areas where the translated questions needed slightly altering. Unfortunately, it was impossible to run any pre-test for the focus groups due to time and logistics that were shifted because of the pandemic.

Limitations to Findings

There will always be risks to the validity and reliability of any given research project, according to Elliston (2011, loc. 2116). These risks suggest limitations upon a research project and need to be taken into consideration. Perhaps the primary risk relating to this project was mentioned above and is what Bernard refers to as the "deference effect or the acquiescence effect" (2006, 241). This is the idea that participants will offer the answers they think the researcher will want to hear or are the right answers for the time.

From my own observation over twenty-five years of residency in the country, Mongolians have a propensity towards this in certain circumstances, especially if the answer reflects upon them as a person and their character. The interview environment in this case is key. To this end, for the cross-cultural missionaries gathered for the security training in Chiang Mai in January 2020, it was at an informal location in the lounge of our accommodation, and for the two remaining sample groups, I hired a private room in one of Ulaanbaatar's popular coffee shops. Each interview began with general conversation, a coffee, tea or something similar, and of course, something to eat. As suggested by Bernard, I stressed that there are no right and wrong answers to the questions I would ask (238). In addition, I had built up considerable relationship currency with many of the participants, especially with the missionaries, over the years and was generally confident of their responses and hopefully able to recognise when an answer leant towards acquiescence so that I could probe with a follow-up question.

Obviously, due to time constraints, COVID, and security issues, this research was unable to encapsulate all of the cross-cultural missionaries sent out from Mongolia. However, the representative samples are a significant proportion of this incredible cross-cultural missionary movement and include most of the key personnel known to me at the time of this research and available for participation.

Reliability and Validity

According to Steinar Kvale (2007, 122), reliability and validity refer to whether the data is consistent and trustworthy and reproducible. They also refer to the correctness and strength of a statement given during the interview. Therefore, the first method of triangulation, and the primary one, was to draw from the distinctiveness of each sample group interviewed. All three sample groups have their individual viewpoint and responsibility within the movement, bringing different perspectives to the same topic. To reflect this, I subtly altered the questions for each sample group. By employing this method, I hoped to bring a sense of consistency and Kvale's sense of correctness and strength to statements given and the data analysis.

Secondly, in both the interviews and focus groups, I recorded the conversations on more than one machine and personally back-translated the transcripts to reduce as much misunderstanding as possible. In attempting what Brinkmann and Kvale label "deliberate naivete" (2014, 33–34), I allowed the participants to answer the questions freely, trying not to add or subtract anything from my own perspective or impose my own presuppositions. Instead, I simply tried to listen and learn and hoped that this would be sufficient to bring a measure of triangulation to the analysis.

To further mitigate the challenge of providing accurate, reliable data, I have also used a method of constant comparison (Gibbs 2007, 96) to check and evaluate the data. Part of this process is to be alert for any negative or unusual statements concerning general topics and to investigate these (96-97). Using MAXQDA as a tool for processing the data, I have dropped memos into the documents to remind me later to pursue certain issues or to note specific themes emerging from the dialogue, consciously or subconsciously. Finally, I have read and reread these interview transcripts many times and have become somewhat familiar with the content. All this is to give the best possible validity and reliability to the data analysis under the current challenging circumstances.

Summary

In this section, I have presented an overview of this research project and discussed the research rationale, identifying the necessary gaps exposed during the literature review. The most significant gap is the sparseness of precedent literature concerning the modern-day Mongolian church or its cross-cultural missionary movement. Therefore, to maximise the information received, semi-structured interviews with open-ended questions were conducted with the three main bodies constituting the Mongolian cross-cultural missionary movement: the missionaries, the sending churches and the sending organisations. These interviews were designed to allow the Mongolians to openly share their own perspective and paint a picture of the movement's current status. In addition, I conducted two focus groups to discuss a couple of the challenges this movement faces. These focus groups also acted as a balance and check for the interviews. Chapter 5 presents my research findings, which are first organised around general categories utilising missiologist Howard Brant's seven essential qualities of an emerging movement from the Majority-World (2009). Second, I present an analysis under four reoccurring themes that emerged from the findings.

Chapter 5

The Findings:
The Current Mongolian Missionary Movement and Paths Forward

Chapter 4 outlined the methodology and challenges that faced the conducting of this research. This chapter will present the research findings by describing the data analysis process before outlining the findings in detail. This data will first be observed through the matrix of Howard Brant's Seven Essentials of Majority-World Emerging Mission Movements (2009) and then analysed under four recurring themes which emerge from the findings. Finally, this chapter will offer some preliminary applications of these findings towards the growth and sustainability of the Mongolian cross-cultural missionary movement.

For the past fourteen years, Howard Brant has served in the capacity of "Champion for New Initiatives in Mission" with Serving In Mission (SIM).[1] He has experienced many emerging mission movements worldwide, primarily focusing on Majority-World nations. His focus has been on those movements in the early stages seeking to discover what it would take for them to take root and develop into stronger missionary movements. His seven essentials are core values of such a movement as he has observed them over the years (Brant 2009). While I acknowledge that these seven essentials may not be all that is required for such a movement to survive and grow, they

---

[1] SIM is an international mission organisation with more than 4,000 workers serving in more than seventy countries. SIM members serve God among many diverse people groups in every continent. www.sim.org/about

present a good first set of foundational pillars from which to analyse the strengths and weaknesses of the Mongolian cross-cultural missionary movement.

The Process of Data Analysis

As mentioned in the previous chapter, the interviews were recorded, transcribed and translated for analysis. Once this process was completed, I uploaded the transcripts onto a computer-assisted qualitative data analysis programme, MAXQDA. Before arriving at this stage, I had listened and observed through the interviews, taking note of first impressions. Later, when reading between the lines of the transcripts, I began placing memos and notes against the various files as I uploaded them onto MAXQDA to help with analysis. Once uploading was completed I began the initial coding starting with Howard Brant's seven essentials (2009) as my initial set of categories before adding additional codes as the analysis continued. Finally, I began to gather the many codes into groups, and from these groups four themes began to emerge: A unity/disunity dichotomy, nomadic lifestyle influences, theological and missiological issues and socioeconomic struggles, and the Korean influence of the Mongolian missionary movement.

Simple identification codes were introduced representing each participant. At no stage in this study are real names given so that participants could be guaranteed confidentiality in this reporting of results. Identification codes used in this study are designated as follows:

- Cross-cultural missionaries are represented by the initials CM and a number signifies the individual.

- Sending church leaders are represented by the initials CL and a number signifies the individual

- Sending agency leaders are represented by the initials SA and a number signifies the individual

- Focus group participants are represented by the initials FG1 or FG2 and a number signifies the individual

For simplicity's sake I have chosen to order the findings in this chapter to reflect the order Brant uses (loc 703-1019) which does not necessarily denote the order or significance of the findings. The strength of the individual elements within the movement will become apparent as the findings unfold below.

Using Brant's Categorisation for Initial Analysis of the Data

This section uses Brant's seven essentials of an emerging Majority-World missionary movement (2009) as a matrix to present an overall analysis of the Mongolian cross-cultural missionary movement. They are: calling, visionary leaders, missional churches, appropriate training, flexible structures, sustainable finances and prayer.

Calling

Calling was one of the strongest elements mentioned throughout the interviews, especially among the missionaries. Furthermore, the sending churches and sending agencies considered it a prerequisite for acceptance of a candidate into mission. In answer to the question "how did you become a missionary?" each of the missionaries tells a story of how God called, confirmed, and sent them to the mission field. It seemed like one of the most straightforward questions for them to answer, and there was a tangible sense of the reality of God's guidance in each story.

Table 1 below records short phrases the respondents made concerning their experiences relating to their calling and highlights different aspects of that calling. In summary, the respondents considered that a calling is from God; it is to be a missionary and often to a specific place or people group.

Table 1: Aspects of The Missionary's Calling

	Expressions of Calling	Aspects of Calling
CM1	At that time, **God said,** "you will serve in your Samaria."	Specific place/people
CM2	But God's calling was **to become a missionary.**	To be a missionary
CM3	God has **prepared a special plan for your life.**	From God
CM4 & 5	**God put a call to missions in our hearts** about ten years ago	From God
CM6 & 7	It seemed like **God was saying,** "B, it is time for your family to go."	From God
CM8	**I am here because He has called me.**	Specific place/people
CM11 & 12	During that time, God clearly revealed that **he was calling us** [to a particular town]	Specific place/people
CM13	I received my **calling to become a missionary** in 2008 when God spoke	To be a missionary
CM14 & 15	Our heart and **our call is for the Russian people.**	Specific place/people

The leaders interviewed from the sending churches desired to see and hear a person's calling before sending them out as missionaries (CL1&2; CL6; CL7). There was an expectancy within the sending churches for those being sent to have some form of calling from God. "We send them based on their calling,"[2] says CL7. And while the

---

[2] As much as possible, all quotations from the participants have been left as they were supplied to me by the translator for authenticity. Only in certain instances have I attempted to alter or tidy up the grammar in order to give clarity.

sending agencies did not particularly articulate their expectancy of a calling, as SA4 explained, "The first step is always to hear their calling." This first essential element reveals a foundational strength among the Mongolian missionaries serving cross-culturally. Personal calling appears to be firmly rooted as one of the foundation elements of the cross-cultural missionary movement from Mongolia.

Visionary Leaders

When considering visionary leaders within the movement, two observations emerge pointing towards a strong underlying theme weaving throughout the interviews. The first observation is the unmistakable sense of unity towards God's call on the movement to reach the Mongol diaspora with the gospel. The second is that although there is a clear direction, a common goal, identifiable leadership within the movement is not as apparent.

Direction

Simply stated, there is oneness on the calling of the Mongolian church to the Mongol diaspora situated in the nations surrounding Mongolia and as far away as Afghanistan, Pakistan, and Turkey. Eight of the participants across the three sample groups referred to the notion of reaching the Mongol diaspora (CM2; CM4; CM8; CL1; CL4; CL7; SA4; SA6).

The Mongol Empire was the world's largest land empire, and Modern Mongolia's national identity is built upon its key figure, Genghis Khan (Encyclopedia Britannica 2020). Today, the area of the former Mongol Empire is populated with Mongol minority people groups as a result of the heydays of the Empire. Therefore, from the early days of the church, Genghis Khan's Medieval Empire has been seen as a framework for taking the gospel out to the nations (Hogan 2014).

CM8 sums it up succinctly when he states, "Everyone agrees that we should return to lands that Chinggis khaan[3] conquered with the gospel . . . we should bring the gospel to diaspora Mongol." Another commented, "Before, we [Mongolia] caused bloodshed, but now we want to reach them with the blood of Jesus; then we invaded them with swords, but now we want to reach them with the sword of the Word of God" (CL4). The directional goal of the movement seemed clear among the respondents to this study.

Leadership

When the missionaries were asked whether they recognised any visionary leadership within the movement (appendix A) the respondents were not as clear with their responses as they were with the direction towards the Mongol diaspora. Although, participants did acknowledge those they deemed as "role models" (CM2; CM3). "They are the people who walk ahead of us and have experienced more than us" (CM2). "I think there are not many who see the big picture," adds CM6. This comment may, perhaps, more accurately reflect an emerging movement in its early days. Addison suggests that leaders or founders should "point the way because they can see the destination" (2011, loc 721), suggesting those "who walk ahead" (CM2) are leaders in the making. The Mongolian church displays a coherent direction but appears unable to identify a particular leader or leaders who currently provide coherent identity and guidance towards the plan of how to reach the Mongol diaspora.

Missional Churches

Questions 3 and 4 of the interview guide for the sending church leadership (appendix B) considered how the church leaders understood the relationship between the

---

[3] This is the transliteration of the spelling of his name in Mongolian Чингэс Хаан, Chinggis Khaan, otherwise I have used the English spelling most commonly found: Genghis Khan

church and mission. Nearly all of the sending church leaders interviewed suggested, at least in part, that they had a grasp of the concept of missional church as table 2 shows. Yet, the wider Mongolian church community, reflected in the cross-cultural missionaries' responses that follow, appears to reflect that their leaders might not have grasped the importance of the place of mission in the life of a church.

Table 2: Sending Church Leaders' Expressions of Missional Church

Sending Church Leaders	Expressions of Missional Church
CL1 & 2	mission is the core of the church.
CL4	A church is not a church unless we do mission.
CL5	all of us are missionaries.
CL6	If there is no mission in a church, then this church is not developed.
CL7	A continuation of Jesus' mission.

CL2, a pastor of a Mongolian congregation in Seoul, South Korea, makes a telling observation from outside of Mongolia.

> The Mongolian churches only see mission as something that a group of people, people with the calling or a mission organisation do. So the church's participation is small. I want them to understand that it is not a mission organisation's work, nor the work of a missionary, but understand the importance of their [own] participation, and participate in it they must. (CL2)

Several cross-cultural missionaries voiced similar concerns; for instance, CM1 believes that "mission is a new understanding for them [the church]." Another commented, "the churches are not supportive," going on to suggest the need to "bring the leaders together to help them understand that now is the time for mission" (CM13).

These comments may point to another potential issue within the current missionary movement: the churches' underdeveloped theology of mission. It may also reflect the influence of the socioeconomic situation on the Mongolian church. Hence, I will discuss these two issues under a single heading later in this chapter.

Appropriate Training

According to the research interviews it is apparent that a significant number of those involved with the missionary movement in Mongolia can trace their calling and understanding back to YWAM in Mongolia and its training courses. YWAM has four bases currently operating across Mongolia. The largest of these is in Erdenet (SA4), the third-largest city in Mongolia and home to one of the first churches whose original pastor is today a cross-cultural missionary and one of the previously referred to role models . All four YWAM bases offer the Discipleship Training School (DTS) and Erdenet offers a School of Biblical Studies (SBS). SA4 explains that these courses are preferred because they are intensive but short. As short-term thinkers (see discussion below under nomadic lifestyle influences), Mongolians respond more positively to shorter and more practical courses such as YWAM offers.

In addition to these YWAM courses, several Bible schools and colleges offer pastoral and theological training courses, while other training centres offer more practical Bible training opportunities (Zylstra 2017). A number of these schools have affiliation with the Asian Theological Association (Asian Theological Association 2021). However, within the confines of the research schedule, I was unable to find details of courses offered in these schools with a specific mission or cross-cultural mission focus. There is the opportunity for further study and consultation with the Bible schools and colleges to amend this apparent lack of available information at the time of writing.

Respondents from sending agencies and sending churches recognise the need for training (SA1; SA5; SA6) and acknowledge that the YWAM bases at least offer generic DTS and SBS courses that are tried and tested worldwide. In addition, InterCP (SA2)[4] offers "Vision School," a training programme introducing participants to the concept of mission. All these are valuable resources. Nonetheless, there is an acknowledged need for more specific biblical and practical training explicitly aimed at cross-cultural mission.

The church leader who articulated this need for missionary training most clearly, CL1, says, "We need to teach them what is a missionary; how to confirm a calling; how to enter into a new culture when on the mission field; how to communicate with a sending church or a mission organisation, etc."

Of course, recognising a need and implementing a solution are two different challenges. To this end, a couple of the agencies in Mongolia have partnered with Pioneers (SA5 & SA7) which began by sending their missionary candidates to practical orientation training in Chiang Mai, Thailand, prior to field placement. CM11 & CM12 commented, "This training opened our eyes . . . this training was a blessing for us." Interestingly, the pandemic lockdowns forced Pioneers' training to shift online and then to move in-country, which is a huge step forward in developing a training program in Mongolia that addresses the relevant cultural issues at hand. Table 6 brings together some of the responses throughout the interviews to the kinds of issues this training might address.

---

[4] InterCP Mongolia, is an extension of InterCP Korea, which in turn is part of InterCP International. www.intercpinternational.org

Table 3: Participants' Comments About Appropriate Training.

Appropriate Training elements	
For the missionaries:	
visa challenges, health care, children's education, how to raise support, how to use support wisely, cultural adaptation, living as a local, not a Mongolian, marriage course, church planting strategies, theological foundations	CL1&2, CM2, CM4, SA1, SA4, SA5
For the churches:	
What is mission? Member care, support issues	SA1, SA4, SA5, CM2, CL7

Flexible Structures

When sharing about the Mongolian cross-cultural missionary movement specifically (appendices A, B, and C), the respondents recognised that this missionary movement is "just starting," "at the early stage," "just beginning," or, taking its "first steps" (SA1; CM4; CM8; CM11). Therefore, it is not surprising that the majority of the agency leaders interviewed are operating using external systems and structures inherited from outside organisations (SA2; SA4) or Western and Korean churches they are currently affiliated with.

There is little evidence of any structure within the churches or the sending organisations that could be recognised as contextually Mongolian. Each has its own independent way of working. On the one hand, CL7 comments, "everyone is different; you [the researcher] and I have different ideas; likewise, every [sending] organisation has a different direction to move in." On the other hand, there is an awareness of the need to come together to move forward in a more comprehensive manner. As SA6 remarks, "We need to sit and talk about how we can make it [the movement] better. It means deciding together. As nomads, this is not a natural process."

As noted earlier, Addison observes, it is the visionary leaders who will rally people and focus them towards a cause (2019, loc. 672). This suggests that the role models highlighted earlier may need to become the catalyst for bringing this movement towards networking together and so towards the next stage of growth as a movement. Currently, the lack of definable structures points towards the young nature of the movement, as was acknowledged in the initial comments at the start of this subsection.

Sustainable Finances

Prior to the COVID pandemic the Mongolian economy had been on a steady upward trajectory for the last couple of years and at the beginning of 2019 stood at roughly 5.8 percent according to a recent World Bank publication (Nganou and Batsuuri 2020). And in Ulaanbaatar, there has been a sense of individual growth and stability on the ground. Yet, from its inception, the church has largely only touched the poorer end of society with a few exceptions. However, much of the economic growth's benefits do not appear to have significantly influenced the Mongolian church. Perhaps the most significant reason for this could be the current demographics of the Mongolian church.

According to more recent research data on the Mongolian church, it appears many of the churches consist largely of students or young people at one end and older, retired adults, often women at the other, with women outnumbering the men two to one (Mongolian Evangelical Alliance 2020). In support of this fact, one of the sending church leaders interviewed describes the demographics of his church, commenting, "Eighty people come to church, but only 30 percent of them give an offering because most of them are young teenagers and students" (CL5). According to another study completed in 2018, children and youth constitute around 45 percent of church attendees in Mongolia (Visser, Byambatseren, and Stephens 2019). Few congregations exist with a balanced mix that includes working adults and families, the young and very old. A significant proportion of young singles and young families find themselves in substantial personal debt as they seek to be successful; in the culture this translates as having their own apartment, a nice car and children in private education. Having an outward appearance of success in modern Mongolia is important (J. Hays 2016).[5]

This financial dilemma leaves the churches feeling the weight of month to month survival. It makes the church's commitment to cross-cultural missionary giving difficult (FG1-1). However, the research highlighted that a few sending churches commit to paying their missionaries' Social Insurance payments as a minimum (CL3; CL4; CL6). This act is a positive step revealing a heart to do all that they possibly can at this time.

From the missionaries' perspective, though they admitted that this situation creates a condition where their home churches cannot commit to regular financial support, there is a boldness in obedience to the calling on their lives. "[Prior to departure] we still had many thoughts about how we would live and our financial situation, but being obedient is a blessing" (CM6). As one solution, many missionaries are currently beginning life on the field as language students. Several respondents have obtained scholarships from their schools of learning in their chosen places of ministry (CM2; CM3; CM14; FG2-3). This scholarship has come with a stipend that supplements their support. However, such stipends can only be a short-term solution to a longer-term need.

All of this paints a picture of a church that is currently only around 1 percent of the population and which believes it does not have sufficient resources in the current financial climate to function as it would desire. The church leaders and sending organisation leaders interviewed indicated that they simply did not have enough money to support their missionaries alone. In truth, most pastors seemed unable to cover the day-

---

[5] This article while not stating specifically the importance of success it reveals the mindset of those with money in modern Mongolia and their need to show their status. For many it is simply the fight to get out of poverty and dependence.

to-day running costs of their church and its weekly programmes (CL4; CL6; CL7; CM11).

This financial situation has led many to seek partnerships, or more accurately, connections, with other wealthier churches (CL5) or missionary organisations in Korea (SA1) or the West, like Mongolian Missionaries Together's[6] (SA5) relationship with Pioneers. This issue raises two questions: how can the various parts of the movement seek strategic partnerships, and how should those partnerships be effectively established?

Prayer

It is worth noting that the first and last of Brant's seven essentials for emerging missionary movements—calling and prayer—for the Mongolians are by far the strongest. These two essential elements, like bookends, undergird this movement of God. I can say with confidence that Mongolians know how to pray. For Mongolian cross-cultural missionaries prayer features as part of their everyday life, in their relationship with God (CM2; CM3; CM8; CM11), in their corporate life on the field as a team (CM1; CM3; CM6), or back home within their sending churches (CM2; CM7; CM8).

The interviews revealed that prayer walking is a strategic part of the preparation for moving into new ministry locations. "We prayer walked in the streets" (CM3). "We prayer walked for five days" (CM12), commented two of the missionaries. Each sending agency interviewed holds regular prayer times for cross-cultural missionaries and mission. "Prayer is the strength of an organisation," says SA2, and the foundation of an organisation, believes SA5, for "If we don't pray, we don't do anything," asserts SA6. Moreover, prayer is one element that draws the whole Christian community together in

---

[6] Mongolian Missionaries Together (MMT) is known by some as the Mongolian Missionary Movement (MMM). However, as a registered organisation the government will not accept "movement" in the title for political reasons. Therefore, they chose a word that translates as "Together." To this end, I have chosen to call them Mongolian Missionaries Together to reflect this.

Mongolia. These interviews revealed an intimacy with God which is foundational for all respondents.

From the participants' responses, it is more than just the importance of prayer that is vital and necessary. Prayer is a component of what I have termed in this research as "intimacy with God"—a close personal relationship with the living God. "God provides for me and directs me, and I lack nothing as I walk by faith" (SA2). God's provision of the participants' needs and prayer requests is evident (SA2; SA6; CM4; CM6; CM14). "God provides for us through his church" (CM5). God also provides through others, as in the case of CM15: "The Lord provides our monthly expenses through various other people."

Summary

I have used Howard Brant's seven essentials of an emerging missionary movement from the Majority-World (2009) as a matrix or framework through which to analyse the current Mongolian cross-cultural missionary movement. Through this process, I have aimed to provide some answers to four field research questions posed in the previous chapter.

1. What are some key elements of a successful and sustainable cross-cultural missionary movement?

2. What are some of the challenges Mongolian missionaries face when ministering in a cross-cultural environment?

3. Can you identify, from your experience, some of the strengths and weaknesses of the current Mongolian missionary movement?

4. How do you understand the relationship between the missionaries, sending churches and the sending organisations involved in this missionary movement?

First, this movement is strongly bookended by the first and the last elements, calling and prayer. There is clarity of calling and direction, giving a sure foundation on which this movement is built, with prayer permeating each stratum of the movement. As a new first-generation movement, there are several essential elements still underdeveloped. Their theology of mission and the place of mission within the church and good structures around which this movement can be built are limited. Partnerships will be a key element in sustaining this missionary movement and helping it find a more secure financial footing, perhaps. The following section will examine four emerging themes providing additional contextual analysis of the Mongolian cross-cultural missionary movement and shed further light on the challenges ahead.

Analysis of Key Research Results

In this section, I will explore four themes that emerged from the analysis of the Mongolian cross-cultural missionary movement. These themes are, first, the unity, disunity dichotomy; second, the influence of the nomadic lifestyle on the development of the movement; third, missiological grounding and the need for a stronger structure; fourth, the foreign influences that mitigate against establishing true indigeneity.

Unity, Disunity Dichotomy

This issue first appeared when respondents were asked to think about the direction of the calling expressed by the movement. On the one hand, there is an evident unity towards a common goal, the desire to reach the Mongol diaspora with the gospel (CM2; CM4; CM8; CL1; CL4; CL7; SA4; SA6). But on the other hand, the lack of coherence in how to accomplish this task is summed up in the phrase "there is no togetherness" (CM7). This problem suggests it is more than a simple deficiency of organisation or lack of strategies.

From the participants' responses, this lack of togetherness is best observed in the relationships between the various parts of the movement. While all the sending church leaders interviewed highlighted the importance of regular, even weekly, communication with their missionaries via social media, the missionaries themselves raised several concerns about the quality and depth of these relationships from their perspective. CM2 comments, "I wouldn't say that the relationship [with the sending church] is close." CM3 finds that communication also becomes distant over distance, i.e.. when on the field. CM4 described his relationship with his pastor as a "ministry relationship, not a close relationship." The relationships between missionaries and sending churches indicate a possible lack of depth. CL1 observed that there is a need for a "relationship of trust."

With all the church leaders interviewed being born and raised during the communist era of pre1991, there is perhaps an unwitting hesitancy to automatically open up. Relationships between the pastors and the missionaries can become awkward. CM8, a younger man of thirty, when on a summer road trip with his pastor in 2019, concluded, "I realised that we are not so close." Instead, it might be defined as a "ministry relationship" rather than a close relationship, as CM4 observed.

There appears to be a strong value placed on independence within the nomadic lifestyle and culture that can affect missionaries' relationships with their supporting churches or partners. According to Mongolian professor Badarch Kherlen (2014, 165), this independence prioritises self-direction and freedom of thought and action and yet, a high relatedness of relationship. This is borne out in the following narrative from CM1:

> The organization told us to leave the country. However, we were not there because someone gave us permission but because God asked us to go . . . . As a team [of Mongolians], we met and prayed together. Whenever we prayed, the Lord said that "it is not the time, and look at Me, but not the storm. Do not focus on the waves; you will start to sink as soon as you see the waves. So look at me." . . . Therefore, we told the organisation that we would not leave the country. On one side, it was hard for us. Because the

organization strictly told us to leave the country . . . our decision was against the organisation's authority. (CM1)

As part of an international mission team, in a sensitive situation for missionaries, these Mongolians were asked to leave their location on safety grounds by the mission. As CM1 explains, they came to their own decision before God, independently of the larger organisation. Naturally, this decision caused difficulties in the partnership relationship.

Below in tables 4 and 5 are some further comments concerning this dichotomy. Table 4 shows the disunity that this independent nature causes while table 5 reveals the participants' desire to be united.

Table 4: Participants' Comments on the Apparent Disunity

Current Disunity and independence	Participant
[Churches are] unable to unite.	SA1
[Bible Schools]. don't participate with each other, or they do not want to participate together	CL3
The Church is far from them [organisations] and independent	CL5
There is no togetherness! The Mongolian Church doesn't understand missionaries	CM6 & 7
It hasn't reached a point where we united [talking about the movement]	CM8
Mongolian missionaries find it impossible to partner together.	CM11 & 12

Table 5: Participants' Comments on the Need for Unity

Desired Unity and relationship	Participant
A movement can go further in unity.	SA2 & 3
All the churches, people and organizations who do mission moving together; that is a movement.	SA5
Many deep and specific things connect when we are united in this vision.	CL17
We need to unite, have a goal, have one vision. . . . Then to move forward in unity, we need to grow the relationship.	CM4 & 5
The whole Mongolian church needs to unite humbly in God's mission vision	CM6 & 7

From these two collections of brief comments, it is apparent that even though there are many areas where there is a lack of coherence and dysfunction in the relationships, there is also a strong desire to move forward and begin working together. This situation suggests a young movement with little structure to support it and one that is influenced by some of its own cultural patterns of life. This leads to the next emerging theme: the nomadic lifestyle's influence on the movement.

Nomadic Lifestyle Influences

In recent years, attempts have been made to determine the cultural values of Mongolia using the six-dimensional model of Geert Hofstede (2010), first by Rarick et al. (2014) and second by Purevdorj et al. (2020). While others have also attempted to do so, in part, the published studies of these two cited works are readily available. Although their findings differ considerably at times, together, they give us a useful insight into the Mongolian mindset (see table 6 below).

Hofstede's six dimensions are (i) Power Distance (PDI) which refers to the degree of acceptance of an inequality in power between employers and employees (2010,60). (ii) Individualism vs. Collectivism (IDV) which measures the strength of the tie between people in society; individualistic—people who are expected to fend for themselves, versus collectivist—societies where the ties are integrated and strong (92). (iii) Masculinity vs Femininity (MAS) indicator shows how society distributes gender roles among men and women. In masculine societies, men are shown to be assertive and prosperous while women are tender and caring, "concerned for the quality of life" (140). (iv) Uncertainty Avoidance Index (UAI) is described simply as "the extent to which the members of a culture feel threatened by ambiguous or unknown situations" (191). (v) Long Term Orientation vs. Short Term Orientation (LTO) simply put is that Long Term Orientation orientates toward the future and long term plans. In contrast, Short Term Orientation is concerned with "fostering virtues related to the past and present," resulting in short-term planning and living in the here and now (239). (vi) Indulgence vs, Restraint (IVR) suggests that indulgent societies encourage members to "act as one pleases, spend money, and indulge in leisure." In contrast, its opposite suggests that members of the society are those who would curb and regulate such indulgence (281).

Table 6: Results of the Two Cultural Values Studies Used for This Analysis.[7]

Method	Date	Researchers	PDI	IDV	MAS	UAI	LTO	IVR
Six dimensions	2020	Purevdorj et al.	85	57	70	28	36	59
Five dimensions	2014	Rarick et al.	18	71	103	92	41	N/A

As nomadic peoples, one of the key results in these studies is Mongolia's Long Term Orientation (LTO) score, which is similar in both studies in table 6. It reveals that Mongolians are short-term thinkers and planners, focusing on the here and now. For

---

[7] Key to table 6: Power Distance Index (PDI), Individualism vs Collectivism (IDV), Masculinity vs Femininity (MAS), Uncertainty Avoidance Index (UAI), Long Term Orientation (LTO), Indulgence vs. Restraint (IVR).

Mongolians, their LTO creates an immediacy as seen in the sense of urgency about getting to the mission field among those called. For example, SA3 comments, "Some churches say that they will send a missionary when they are equipped well, but we say, go when you are young." Another respondent (SA5) shares that her own early experience as a young cross-cultural missionary was that once the decision was made, she quit midway through her college studies and went. This sense of urgency has created tension between missionaries and their sending churches, and even for the sending agencies. Once called, there is a need to go; being prepared appears to take a back seat in decisions at this time.

One of the beneficial influences of the nomadic lifestyle, though, is their incredible ability to travel from point A to point B with relative ease. CM14 comments,

> We prayed and decided I would go first to see. Then I went there and spent twelve days [on the trip]. It takes five days to reach K from Mongolia [overland]. I got there, met with the school and returned to Mongolia, spending another five days on the journey.

In this statement, he revealed that he had just two days to spend in the chosen country and city to accomplish everything in preparation for returning as a family. This example reveals the Mongolians' tenacity and ability to travel vast distances (in this case, 3600 kms) with limited resources. I have heard this kind of story and journey spoken of many times with the Mongolians over the time I have served in this country. Very rarely are tickets for such a journey purchased in advance.

As for other cultural values, Mongolians appear as individualists, according to the IDV scores of fifty-seven and seventy-one (Purevdorj, Bolormaa, and Kh 2020, 1246; Rarick et al. 2014, 4) suggesting that an individual's rights and responsibilities may be placed over those of the societal groups, or as in CM1's example above, the organisation's. In other words, the immediate needs in any given situation are more relevant and will demand their attention at that moment. From the sending church's perspective this can be seen when three participants (CL5; CL6; CM14) admitted that pressing financial issues at home in Mongolia took precedence over the financial support of its cross-cultural missionaries. "Our church stopped supporting us due to financial hardships that they have," said one respondent (CM14). The missionary exhibited no malice when making this statement, simply an empathetic acceptance of the reality of the situation. In Focus Group 2, this situation was talked about as a matter of fact for pastors with limited resources. "Finance is a difficult subject to discuss," said FG2-2 in the middle of a discussion. Being a high power distance society, the Mongolian missionaries, while talking openly in the focus group on a common subject would be reluctant to discuss their finances directly with their church leadership, feeling a sense of shame that they need to do so. Further discussions would have been extremely useful on this topic, but unfortunately the Mongolian Health Ministry restrictions prevented this possibility at the time.

Other issues also become affected by this sense of short-term planning, immediacy, and independence. Two that deserve a brief note are the education of children on the mission field and the healthcare of the missionaries on the mission field.

Children's Education

This topic was discussed in one of the focus groups. Education is an important factor in Mongolian thinking, a value installed in them during their years under communist rule (Educational International 2019).[8] During Mongolia's thirty years of independence, there has been an abundance of international and private schools established in several languages, but homeschooling has yet to be considered as an

---

[8] Educational International (EI) is an organisation which aims to further the cause of organisations of teachers and education employees worldwide https://www.ei-ie.org/.

option. Homeschooling is still frowned upon by the government authorities, even seen as possibly seditious (FG1-1).

Consequently, moving cross-culturally as a family brings difficulties for those with school-age children. Options are limited. "Mongolia needs to be ready for all these [educational] demands," suggested CM12. Even as a recognised dilemma, there are no easy answers which do not involve large sums of money or the learning of English. Those currently with school-age children revealed that they have adapted to what is available to them in their locations (CM6&7; CM8; CM11&12; CM14&15). The education of cross-cultural missionaries' children is a topic that needs to be thought through at some stage for the future sustainability of the missionary movement.

Each of the parents involved in the focus group shared their story of the educational challenges for their children on the field. First, it is worth noting how many only thought about the issues once they arrived on the field, echoing the nomadic short-term orientation to planning and immediacy mentioned earlier. Perhaps the single biggest challenge discussed was how to keep the children registered in the school system in Mongolia when they go to the mission field. Recognition of the issue is a huge step towards finding suitable resolutions, and some participants of the focus group expressed interest and desire to continue exploring options in this area.

Healthcare

Healthcare costs were mentioned as another important topic for Mongolian cross-cultural missionaries. Four current missionaries and one former missionary couple (CL1 & CL2) mentioned experiencing serious health issues while serving on the field. One respondent commented, "Because I didn't think I would get sick, I did not have health insurance" (CM1). Another simply responded, "I had an unexpected health issue" (CM7). Both of these were of a serious nature. Short-term thinking enters here as CM7 said prior to her comment, "I am not a person who plans; I adjust accordingly to the situations as they arise." Connected to this, nine missionaries (three couples and three singles) commented on the limited financial support while on the field. CM14 commented, "There is no one who consistently supports us. Financially we struggle each day, although we are learning to cope." CM6 commented on their sending churches financial support when he said, "They don't support us each month financially. As I remember, they have financially helped us twice since we left for the mission field." Again, the matter-of-fact manner in which these statements are made supports the 2020 cultural analysis' weak UAI score of twenty-eight suggesting "a tolerance for ambiguity and chaos" (Hofstede, Hofstede, and Minkov 2010, 217). The financial struggle of both sending church and missionary partly relates to the discussion in the section below titled Theological and Missiological Issues and Socioeconomic Struggles.

While important to Westerners, health insurance is not prioritised in the same manner for the Mongolians. Living in the here and now they do not appear to project forward to a time when they might be ill. Organisations and churches will need to consider this when structuring the future sustainability of the movement. In the short term, several missionaries noted that while they are overseas, their churches at least meet the basic Mongolian requirement of Social Insurance (CM3; CM6; CL6). This payment grants them entry into the Mongolian health system when they return. However, neither CM1 nor CM7 were in a place to return and required immediate healthcare. Therefore, building health care contingency funding into the Mongolian cross-cultural missionary movement is a necessary point for future discussion.

Structural Weaknesses and Missiological Grounding

At first glance, it might seem odd to bring these two issues together but it is important to remember that this is a first-generation movement emerging from a first-generation church. Therefore, many of the issues raised by the research participants thus far relate to this fact including the lack of structure and the movement's missiology. Consequently, I will give a brief structural analysis to identify potential areas of weakness using two particular methods of analysis; first, Adizes' lifecycle model in *Managing Corporate Lifecycles* (2014), followed by Bolman and Deal's four frames of reference in *Reframing Organizations* (2013). I will follow with considering the theological and missiological issues.

Adizes' Lifecycle Analysis

Business consultant Ichak Adizes (2017, loc. 583) suggests from the beginning that every system, breathing or not, has a lifecycle and that as they grow and change, they progress through that lifecycle. For over thirty years, Adizes has developed his lifecycle theory and the analytical tools to identify the approximate position of an organisation, company or even tentatively a missionary movement along the lifecycle.

Adizes uses four managerial roles that he believes are necessary for organisations to be effective and efficient. These are Purposeful Performance (P), Administration (A), Entrepreneurial (E), and Integrative roles (I) (loc. 3608). These roles are developed one by one and introduced into an organisation in a particular order throughout its growth (loc. 3619). This section applies his theory to the Mongolian cross-cultural missionary movement to ascertain its place in its lifecycle.

The research data suggests that the Mongolian cross-cultural missionary movement currently displays the following combination of Adizes' four roles. The movement lies somewhere between a dominant P role with the other three operating as subsidiaries (Paei), indicating Infancy on the lifecycle, and a dominant P with a growing E role with the other two as subsidiaries (PaEi), implying it is entering the Go-Go stage of growth as shown by figure 3 below.

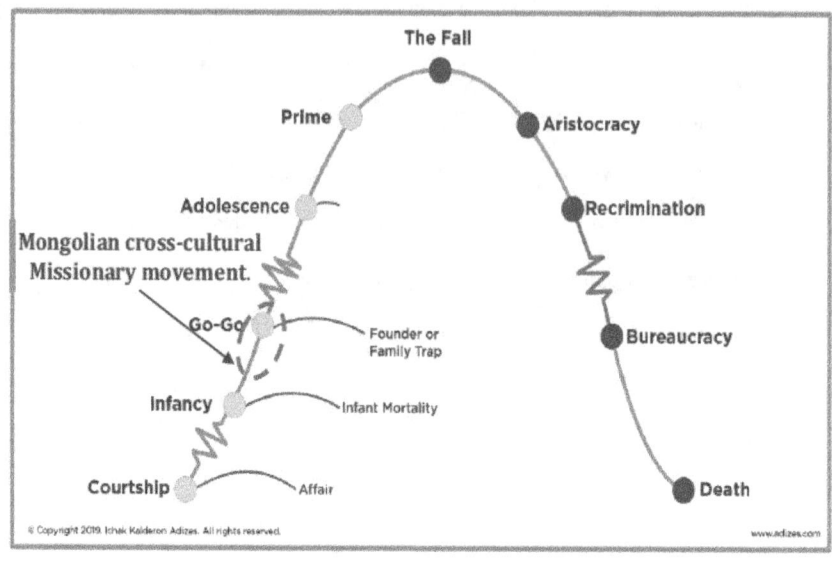

Figure 3: Adizes Lifecycle diagram as Applied to the Mongolian Cross-cultural Missionary Movement.
(adapted from Adizes Institute Worldwide 2019)

Purposeful Performance Role (P)

The Purposeful Performance (P) is the origin of any organisation or movement. As Adizes points out, "every organisation must have a reason to exist" (loc. 3645). For this purpose people come together and decide how to accomplish the task identified. For example, there is a common goal within the Mongolian cross-cultural missionary movement: to reach the Mongol diaspora with the gospel message. In part, this strong P role can also be presumed as the movement is a direct response to the call of God, through Jesus Christ, on all his followers in Matt 28:19-20. Therefore, the words of Jesus Christ contained in these verses clearly define the movement, giving focus to the what of their calling and to whom.

Administrative Role (A)

The Administrative role (A) considers how this might happen and what is needed to make the right things happen in the correct sequence to achieve the task within the right timeframe (loc. 3740). This is the beginning of organisational structure.

Within the current Mongolian missionary movement there appears to be minimal organisational structure or policies and procedures. Much of the mechanism that makes this first-generation movement currently function is borrowed from other international organisations or affiliated churches, as previously noted above (see "Flexible Structures"). According to Adizes, organisations in Infancy lack an A representation, thereby often operating in a "management by crisis" mode (loc. 1364), as seen with the healthcare crisis written above. Travel expenses, faithful financial support and planning for the children's schooling could also fall into this category.

Entrepreneurial Role(E)

The Entrepreneurial role (E) is the place of creativity in an organisation that envisions the future and, in part, how to get there. Those who are prepared to take a risk and not wait until all is in place instead lead the way (loc. 3753). These would include the role models mentioned earlier and potentially those leading the movement.

The Mongolian nomadic lifestyle means they tend to adapt to situations experienced along their individual missionary journeys. This resourcefulness lays the foundation for and fuels their E elements. In turn, it has led some individuals to begin to think strategically and establish an organisation, the Mongolian Mission Partnership (MMP), to support the movement and create an environment where this kind of thinking can be achieved (SA4; SA5; SA6). As I write this, MMP is in the process of officially registering in Mongolia.

Integration Role (I)

Integration (I) is the role that develops a team of necessary people and creates an interdependency across all of the other roles (loc. 3790-3830). Adizes sums it up thusly: it is "that internal sense of belonging. And it is integration that makes an organization efficient" (loc. 3889).

At the current stage of growth (late Infancy/early Go-Go), the I role is by default not developed according to Adizes (loc. 1642). It usually grows as the A role grows. Perhaps the initiation and development of MMP indicates the initial emergence of this role within the movement. As SA6 remarks, "We need to sit and talk about how we can make it [the movement] better. It means deciding together. As nomads, this is not a natural process."

This introduces questions about what the next stage might be and how a missionary movement might continue to move along its lifecycle into and beyond the Go-Go stage of life. As an organisation or movement reaches this stage, momentum generated from early achievements can pull them into many directions (loc. 1305), and opportunities drive the organisation (loc. 1338). This is an important stage where the Mongolian cross-cultural missionary movement will constantly need to morph and restructure as they mature and grow (loc. 1448). Chapter 6 will discuss some next steps to ensure the continued growth towards sustainability, helping the movement into the next lifecycle stage.

Analysis Through Bolman and Deal's Four Frames

Having established where the movement resides on Adizes' lifecycle, it is valuable to view it from other perspectives gaining a multi-dimensional picture of its strengths and weaknesses. I will use Bolman and Deal's seminal work entitled *Reframing Organizations* (2013) to achieve this multi-dimensional picture. Bolman and Deal offer four frames, or lenses, through which to analyse, understand and eventually, if necessary, reframe an organisation (5). While certain frames may be more specific to this project than others, looking through all four provides a fuller picture. Before looking at the movement through each frame of reference, I will briefly summarise Boleman and Deal's descriptions of their four frames.

The Structural Frame: This frame is concerned with the structural composition of an organisation. For example, how the work divided, and who coordinates the organisation's work, or in this case, the movements (49).

The Human Resources Frame: This frame focuses on the organisation as a community of people and "on the fit between human needs and the organizational requirements" (113).

The Symbolic Frame: This frame is concerned with the organisational culture and focuses on how the human element of the organisation, or movement, makes sense of the organisational world in which they operate. These include myths, visions, rituals, and stories that define the organisation for the members (244).

The Political Frame: This frame is about who has authority and how that authority might be used. Bolman and Deal say, "Organizations are coalitions composed of individuals and groups with enduring differences who live in a world of scarce resources. That puts power and conflict at the center of the organizational decision making" (204).

Structural Frame

As a first-generation movement it is not unusual that there is little evidence of structure. While some of the sending churches and sending agencies' legal documentation suggests a semblance of internal organisation, the connection between documentation and practical outworking appears absent. The present movement's insufficient structural framework intertwined with the Mongolian value of their nomadic lifestyle's independent nature is at the root of much of the struggles in communication and the subsequent misunderstandings between the churches, agencies and the missionaries.

According to Bolman and Deal, designing a structure should focus on four aspects: desired ends, the nature of the environment, the talents of the workforce, and the available resources (56). The Mongolian cross-cultural missionary movement's desired end, to reach the Mongol diaspora with the gospel message, is a strong element, and the missionaries (workforce) are passionate and called. However, the environment necessary for missionaries to function on the mission field, team structures, communication networks, etc., are not yet sufficiently formed. As one respondent observed, "We are just beginning. We need to learn from others so we can find some structures" (CM11). Finally, there is a scarcity of resources available to the movement. These deficiencies alone make the movement's sustainability fragile and necessitate partnerships with larger organisations or national churches. In recognition of a lack of experience, CM8 said, "That is why we need to partner with an [international] organisation."

Human Resource Frame

Paradoxically, even though Mongolians seem to have a strong independent element emanating from their nomadic history, the Mongolian culture is built and functions around relationships. As a nation in transition, scoring somewhere in the middle of Hofstede's IDV index (2010), their collective element comes to the fore. As Hofstede et al. remind us, in a collective society, "the personal relationship prevails over the task" (2010, 123). This frame highlights the relationships between people and their organisation, particularly observing how well these two elements fit together (Bolman and Deal 2013, 135).

Observation shows, on the one hand, that there is a sense of family within the movement. This is seen in Mongolians' support and unity during times of crisis, as mentioned by several participants. However, on the other hand, a number of the missionaries expressed concern at not having a sense of family with their sending churches (CM1; CM2; CM4; CM9 & 10). There may be several reasons for this relationship breakdown.

First, it could be partly due to the problem of trust, alluded to earlier in the Unity/Disunity Dichotomy section above. This would suggest a need for both to better understand and appreciate one another's perspective on the place of mission within the church. As CM1 commented, "Because they [the sending church] do not understand my situation, I do not think about trying to meet with them." This tension could suggest that the ecclesiology and missiology necessary to strengthen and sustain the cross-cultural missionary movement has not yet been fully developed, as considered in part I.

Second, the issue of security surrounding some of the locations these missionaries minister in affects and limits communication between the sending church and the missionary. Yet, communications across the movement have been primarily through social media groups, such as Facebook Messenger, WhatsApp, Signal etc., all of which are readily available when used in conjunction with a VPN. The strongest of these groups is among the cross-cultural missionaries themselves.

Bolman and Deal comment that organisation—movements—or more specifically—sending churches—need people and people also need organisations (135). In this instance, there appears to be a need for an appreciation of one another's part or place within the movement, particularly within the relationship between the sending church and the missionary. Whatever the reason for this disconnect with the sending church, this issue ultimately resulted in miscommunication, misunderstanding, and strained relationships.

While the above discussion remains true, there is a noticeable egalitarian approach to overall governance within the cross-cultural missionary movement, exemplified recently in the Mongolian mission forum.⁹ The importance of empowerment was displayed during the discussions when everyone present was encouraged to participate. Apart from using age-respective pronouns, everyone in the movement was on first name terms. Social media, once more, played an integral part in this style of governance and is the principal vehicle for disseminating prayer requests and news across the movement regardless of status.

Irrespective of some of the hierarchical approaches to the leadership within a few of the individual sending churches, these factors potentially offer a degree of levelling across the movement. This egalitarian approach can only help with some of the more tense relationships between some of the sending churches and their missionaries, expressed during the interview stage of this research. However, it is important to remember that much of the breakdown and miscommunication issues relate to this first-generation missionary movement's still-forming structural framework.

The Symbolic Frame

Christianity is a movement full of symbolism. As an expression of Christianity, the Mongolian cross-cultural missionary movement naturally shares many of those same symbols offering a firm spiritual foundation for the movements' contextual framework. In addition, embedded in their shared history Mongolian cultural symbols, centred around Genghis Khan, give the Mongolians a bond and open relationships with the Mongol minorities dispersed across the former Mongol Empire.

Bolman and Deal note, "A vision offers mental pictures linking historical legend and core precepts to future events" (250). While research participants necessarily

---

⁹ These mission forums have been held twice a year in the last couple of years. They are an all-day event open to those involved in cross-cultural mission from the Mongolian church. I have been privileged to attend the last two and am involved in the Mongolian Mission Partnership (MMP) who are responsible for organising these events. These comments are from my own observations when attending these events.

identified no one visionary or group of visionaries as the main leaders within the movement, a strongly defined vision became clear when viewed through the symbolic frame: the call to take the gospel to all the diaspora Mongol peoples. The former Mongol Empire is a shared historical link and a significant symbol for the movement. Coupled with the fact that many among the diaspora have never before heard the name of Jesus, the cultural and Christian symbolism combine to powerfully fuel and motivate this movement. Everyone involved shares a common purpose with a vision for the future (250).

Prayer, as already noted, is a powerful element (ritual) within the Mongolian cross-cultural missionary movement. Many have seen God repeatedly work on their cross-cultural journey, as represented by the testimonies of answered prayer mentioned earlier in this chapter. If, as Bolman and Deal also suggest (256), rituals anchor us to a centre, then prayer firmly anchors this movement in God and God's mission.

Political Frame

As a first-generation movement, the scarcity of and competition for available resources such as finances, structures, available leaders, and expertise creates inevitable friction among this young movement's participating bodies. Typical disputes centre around financial needs versus available resources or the church's needs versus the missionaries' calling, causing stress and sometimes a sense of shame for the decision-maker when choosing between one or the other. This dilemma gives importance and urgency to the currently forming MMP. However, as Bolman and Deal state, harmony, understanding, and progress are possible when each party shares the same values, beliefs, and cultural ways (190).

Theological, Missiological and Socioeconomic Struggles

As pointed out in chapter 2, Paul Hiebert believes that it takes until the third or fourth generation for an indigenous church to truly self-theologise and that without it, there can be no true self-missiologising (Hiebert 1985, 96–97). The literature review gave credence to this when it considered the missionary movements emanating from Africa, Asia, and Latin America. Each has passed through this watershed moment, and each has eminent indigenous theologians. Mongolia still needs to see indigenous theologians grappling with Scripture from a Mongolian point of view. But it is still a church in the transition stage from first to second-generation.

The Mongolian church's underdeveloped theology of mission is supported by comments from a couple of missionaries, which state, "We have a desire to go but feel powerless because the churches are not supportive" (CM13). Or "the church is lacking information about mission, and mission is a new understanding for them" (CM1). Yet, according to statistical research completed on the Mongolian church in 2015 by the Mongolian Evangelical Alliance (MEA), out of 544 church pastors/leaders 191 have a theological degree (MEA 2015, 18). Perhaps too, the country's socioeconomic situation influences this lack of education. The macro socioeconomic climate within Mongolia and the subsequent micro socioeconomic climate within the church can furnish further insight into the lack of church involvement in cross-cultural mission. One leader says in this challenging economic environment, "It seems hard for the Mongolian Church to be outward-looking" (SA6).

Mongolia's first-generation pastors were towards the end of their educational years under communism when the system collapsed and gained independence. "In 1990, life became difficult. Communism dissolved. I finished high school, and there was no university, no job. So, I was on the streets," comments CL3. Hope appeared to leave Mongolia along with communism.

It was cross-cultural missionaries to Mongolia that brought fresh hope in the form of the gospel message, and God raised up Mongolian leaders who today are established pastors within the church. However, a significant number have not completed education beyond high school.[10] In contrast, their children's generation has greater educational opportunities before them at the state level or in a private capacity and from a theological perspective. Thus, the Mongolian church's sphere of influence has primarily been the lower socioeconomic elements of society, reflecting its beginning and the first generation of leaders.

CL4, one such pastor who emerged from Mongolia's transition to independence, makes this observation, "Financially, the Mongolian economy is weak" (CL4). Yet his church is one of the larger, well-established churches with around 200 regular attendees. The church, however, struggles to make ends meet. Like many young people from the early 90s he was forced to find alternative means of daily survival, leading to his involvement in gangs, crime, and prison, a situation that at least two of our participating pastors experienced.

> At that time, society was difficult and poor. Growing up without a father as an orphan influenced me badly, especially without a father. At the age of seventen I was imprisoned because I was on the street; I joined a gang, drinking alcohol, and thieving. (CL4)

And

> At first, I went to a youth meeting and heard about a wise man and a foolish man . . . . When I heard that sermon, it hit me hard in the heart. Then I decided to come again with my friend. But at that time in 2000, people used to see Christianity as a foreign religion, and there was much persecution and opposition. Also, I had many street friends, and it was difficult to leave them. I thought I would leave the church when I had got what I needed. My family situation was very hard. At that time, alcoholic fathers beating their wives and orphaned kids was society's norm. (CL5)

---

[10] Mongolian education system has slowly shifted from a 10-year system (4+4+2) to an 11-year system (5+4+2), and then to a 12-year system (5+4+3) in line with international standards (Asian Development Bank 2017).

These two stories from sending church leaders, ten years apart, tell of a similar journey. Most of the Mongolian church's male and female leaders have a sure and steadfast faith, but not always a rounded theological background from which to teach, only an intimate relationship with God from which to lead. They may believe in mission and have a grasp of missional concepts personally but appear to struggle to impart these ideas to their respective congregations with biblical reference. In light of these findings, it is important that theological and missiological training be made available so that churches can better understand and participate in the *misso Dei*.

The Korean Influence on the Movement

The Korean missionary influence is a theme that runs through this whole research project. This section will examine how much and in what ways the Korean missionaries to Mongolia have influenced the Mongolian church and the missionary movement directly and indirectly. In 1991, South Korean missionaries came to Mongolia through God's call to bring the gospel to the nation. Several of the participants' churches can trace their roots to these early Korean missionaries (CL5; SA1; CL3; CM6; CM14). Generally, Korean missionaries do not stay long-term in Mongolia but leave a definite sphere of influence through their ministry.

The Korean influence on the Mongolian participants in this research appeared to be mixed from what was shared. On a positive note, SA6 notes, "There was a Korean missionary in my church; he encouraged us to pray for mission . . . . He influenced us." And again, SA5, "In 2000-2001, I got an opportunity to study at InterCP's Vision School in Korea." Both comments are from Mongolians significantly involved with sending agencies. But not all influence has been positive, according to a few of the participants (SA2&3; CL6). Sadly, Korean missionaries were sometimes seen as not particularly culturally sensitive. Instead, it would seem that Korean missionaries imported their own dominant church culture into any given situation. Korean missiologist Steve Moon best defines this danger as "inappropriately imposing denominational patterns in a mission field" (2003, 12).

Several of those interviewed have experienced this cultural rub when attempting to move out from under such defined relationships or forward, to the next level, with Korean colleagues (SA5; CL5; CL6). In an indirect example of the influence of the Korean missionaries on the Mongolian church, CL5 had made a personal decision to use his business degree to find a way to support himself and the church, as, at the time, the church was financially unable. However, during our conversation he noted that the church leadership and members felt strongly that he should not work in business as a pastor. He was considered wrong to think about doing this thing. CL6 observes,

> I think Koreans teach that churches must live by their offerings; they shouldn't do business. But Europeans and Americans teach that churches can do business.

Korean missionaries had started CL5's church; therefore, the church had an overwhelming belief that the leader should not work in business. Full-time in the pastorate means trusting the Lord to provide. CL6 observed that "those churches influenced by Korean missionaries are happy when the [Korean] missionary comes [to Mongolia] and gives them money." But this creates an outside dependency. In a separate incident, CL6 told of a disagreement he had with a Korean partner due to their different views on handling finances, eventually parting company and leaving a broken relationship. These insights support Moon's comments about the importation of the missionaries' culture into the host nations (12).

This sense of control from the Koreans that Mongolians felt comes from a strong hierarchical Korean church structure that apparently has unsettled the Mongolian church. Instead, The Mongolian nomadic lifestyle prefers freedom with a measure of independence in their decision-making process. CM5 shared an example of this dilemma.

Before going to the mission field, CM5 was a pastor for twelve years of a particular church. SA1 explains,

> CM5 thought that they [the Mongolian church] supported him, but the Korean [parent] church said, "It is our church; you were a pastor of the church. If you go to the mission field, then we will find a [new] pastor for the church and take care of it in the future." CM5 was shocked when he heard that the church wasn't his. (SA1)

It must also be reported here that in many amazing ways God has used the Korean missionary movement to establish, bless and influence the Mongolian church, in many cases quite positively. While the Korean influence in the initial stages of Christianity in Mongolia has been significant, inevitably over time through cultural misunderstanding, relationships with a few participants in this research project seem to have been damaged (SA5; SA6). Equally, in my observation these young, passionate, and free-spirited Mongolians have also failed in their enthusiasm to understand the Korean perspective. Thus, sadly, at least two of the participants had severed their ties with Korean workers due to these cultural and contextual misunderstandings. Contextualisation and cultural acquisition need to work in both directions for a lasting and deep relationship. This is true in all cross-cultural situations, not just with Koreans.

Summary

In this chapter, I have outlined and sought to understand the current cross-cultural Mongolian missionary movement primarily from the interviews conducted and from the focus group discussions among the participants: the missionaries, the sending churches, and the sending agencies. I have used Howard Brant's seven essentials for such a movement (Brant 2009) as a matrix or framework to accomplish the initial overall analysis before considering four themes that emerged from that analysis. Some key findings were as follows.

First, this movement is strongly bookended by Brant's (2009) first and the last essential elements of calling and prayer. There is a clarity of calling, giving a sure foundation on which this movement is built, and prayer permeates each stratum. There is a consensus among those across the movement that its common goal is to reach the Mongolian diaspora with the gospel using Genghis Khan's former empire as a road map. Yet, how to achieve this agreed goal appears not so coherent. As one participant commented, "There is no togetherness" (CM7). From this insight emerged the first theme that weaves through the research: a lack of coherence. This lack is typified by a disunity/unity dichotomy.

This dichotomy appears to be partially linked to an apparent absence of strong indigenous visionary leadership, as Brant and others understand leaders should be (2009, loc. 762; Addison 2019, loc. 721); rather, those with vision tend to be those going out to the field as role models. Furthermore, cultural worldview issues have made the Mongolians independent people who prefer short-term planning, prioritising the here and now. Sometimes, these traits lead to putting individual preferences above the group. Other elements of concern are a lack of substantial and contextually relevant structure within the movement which, while recognised as being in the early stages (SA1; CM4; CM8; CM11), struggles with weak and tentative relationships in the effort to accomplish the movement's purpose. Cultural influences also limit trust, resulting in a reluctance to establish deep relationships or accountability among missionaries and sending partners. Together with the church's socioeconomic composition, these have helped form this lack of coherence within the fledgling movement.

Another observation is the weak or underdeveloped theology of mission within the churches in Mongolia. Church leaders interviewed articulated missional concepts when sharing about the role of mission in the church, yet without evidencing the outworking of those comments in the church. This situation seems to have created a focus on an inward-looking church rather than an outward-looking one when coupled with the sending churches' socioeconomic position.

Further, the findings give some credence to Hiebert's notion that it can take until the third or fourth generation to truly self-theologise and self-missiologise (1985, 196–97). This research has been conducted in a church transitioning from first to second-generation. The participants have an unspoken sense of reaching for something tangible yet, not quite attainable. Since Hiebert's observations, whether technological advances in communication and the influences of globalisation can affect a faster process than three or four generations remains to be seen.

The final point of note is the significance of the Korean missionary influence in the church and upon the missionary movement. While it has not always been a positive influence, Korean missionaries are responsible for birthing many good churches and organisations. The influence of the Korean missionaries on Mongolia has the potential to be a research topic of its own.

Part III will outline the implications of these findings and present a model for strengthening one specific relationship within the movement, which, together with the newly forming MMP, could potentially be adapted for use where other relationships need encouragement and strengthening. It is hoped this strategic plan will begin the change process for the movement to become more Mongolian in shape and direction.

Part III

Moving Forward: Growing and Sustaining a Cross-Cultural Missionary Movement

In part III, based upon the literature review and the data analysis findings, I intend to show that strengthening key relationships within this fledgling movement in partnership with MMP is the most natural way to grow and sustain this movement. In chapter 6, I develop a strategic plan to strengthen the movement towards a stronger future, and in the final chapter, I will present my conclusions, implications beyond Mongolia, and recommendations.

Chapter 6

Implications of the Findings and Necessary Changes to Grow and Sustain This Movement

Part II considered the methodology used in this research (chapter 4) and analysed the findings of the research process, underscoring some of the strengths and weaknesses of the Mongolian cross-cultural missionary movement (chapter 5). This chapter is divided into four parts: three main sections followed by a brief consideration of the timeframe for this proposal. Section one summarises the journey thus far and shows how the research findings indicate possibilities for addressing some of the weaknesses by utilising some of the movement's strengths to affect growth towards a sustainable future. Section two looks more closely at some of the implications of the research findings. Finally, based upon the above implications, section three outlines and develops a strategic plan of change designed to strengthen and grow the Mongolian cross-cultural missionary movement.

Recognising from the research results the fragility of the relationship between the constituent bodies within this movement, I will focus on what I consider the most strategic of these relationships, that between the sending churches and the sending agencies. I intend to show how this could be best achieved by working in partnership with the newly formed MMP. This last section is divided into two subsections; the first explains the various groups of people involved in this proposed plan and considers their possible and perceived responses, and in the second, I unfold the proposed strategic plan itself.

Discoveries That Point the Way Forward

The literature review revealed a scarceness of material available on the modern-day Mongolian church and its burgeoning cross-cultural missionary movement. This lack is primarily due to the first-generational nature of the Mongolian church. However, the literature review also highlighted certain essential elements necessary for the growth of indigenous missionary movements from the Majority-World. Case studies from Africa, Latin America and Asia in chapter 2 revealed how a nation's history both secular and Christian and its cultural influences affect the development of such an indigenous movement. On a positive note, the research findings revealed that this young, flourishing movement has a clear and passionate, unified goal of reaching across the historical Mongol Empire with the good news of the gospel. This includes Afghanistan, China, many Central Asian nations, Nepal, Siberia, and Turkey.

The Mongolian cross-cultural missionary movement is a first-generation movement emerging from a first-generation Mongolian church. In the early 2000s, a little over a decade after the establishment of the church in modern-day Mongolia, Mongolian indigenous missionaries with a desire to see the wider Mongol family reached with the gospel began to travel to other lands. Since then, it has steadily grown with its vision and sense of calling to take the good news of Jesus Christ throughout the once vast Mongol Empire. Indeed, a missionary movement was birthed.

For historical and religious reasons, many of the countries where Mongol minority peoples reside have gradually become hostile towards missionary activity, especially towards Western missionaries. However, many indigenous people in these nations consider Mongolians to be kinsmen and are warm and welcoming towards them as a race, opening effective doors for the gospel. Though this is a young missionary movement the Mongolian nomadic character and worldview grants them the ability to live and minister among these scattered peoples.

Inevitably, growth brings challenges and causes growing pains on multiple levels for young movements like the Mongolian missionary movement. As shown in the findings of this research among current Mongolian cross-cultural missionaries, these challenges have allowed different personalities and opinions concerning the way forward to surface. These have led to a measure of internal stress and relational strain causing a breakdown in communication and relationship between individuals and within the various parts of the movement.

What the Mongolian cross-cultural mission movement seeks to achieve is innovative and pioneering. Once missionary-receiving nations, like Mongolia, now find themselves sending cross-cultural missionaries out to others around the world. However, simply applying traditional Western methodology and practice to this new movement is proving stultifying. It is like attempting to fit a round peg in a square hole from a contextual standpoint. For example, there are established international missionary teams in some of these nations. For Mongolian missionaries seeking to serve in those countries, these teams would make a good foundation for cooperative missionary outreach and community. However, in order to be accepted some Mongolian missionaries have been asked to complete the same training modules as the team's other members or have the same level of financial support. Speaking from a personal point of understanding as a long-time member of one of these organisations, I recognise that these trainings are often valuable but designed for Western mindsets, often requiring a financial commitment to attend, usually at a more well-established mobilisation base. These requests are simply impossible for Mongolians to comply with due to financial constraints, and the training asked for is often, at present, only available in English.

In an interview with Tod Bolsinger at Fuller in 2014, Juan Martinez stated that "Majority-World leaders have the intuition and experience to continually adapt, to continually experiment and not be surprised when things don't work" (Bolsinger 2018,

198). Like these Majority-World leaders, the leading lights of this cross-cultural missionary movement with a little encouragement have the adaptive capacity to create new systems and structures that will enable Mongolian believers to fulfil their God-given mission in new and innovative ways, rather than being tied to existing and often constricting structures.

Finally, the restricting of international travel for many, including Mongolians, in the past couple of years has providentially provided an opportunity for the movement to pause, to gather, and to reflect on what God has accomplished thus far. As a result, those involved with the Mongolian cross-cultural missionary movement are now prayerfully contemplating how to readjust where needed and beginning to plan for a more cohesive and better-coordinated future. Fittingly, this desire and willingness to recognise and address the movement's challenges lends itself to the findings of this research and to the proposed application of building a stronger and integrated movement.

Implications of the Findings

As observed throughout this dissertation, this movement has been shaped by cultural and historical influences, yet it is also a young, passionate, and focused movement. However, the rapid growth rate, the absence of structural organisation, and the lack of time for missiological reflections leave the movement vulnerable. This is the moment when the Mongolian cross-cultural missionary movement will either grow strong and continue to flourish or the moment it could all dissipate. Relationships within the movement are naturally strained as the different component bodies discover their roles, learn how these roles overlap and explore how to partner together. Figure 4 below pictorially represents the current parts of the movement functioning ideally as an integrated missionary movement. This picture illustrates the goal of this study to see an integrated sustainable missionary movement growing strong.

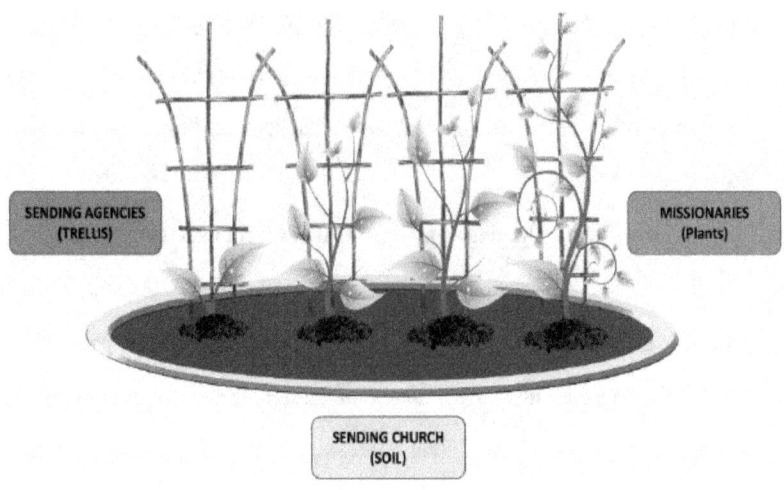

Figure 4: An Integrated Cross-Cultural Missionary Movement

When these three entities integrate, communicate, relate, and serve one another, the movement will be strengthened and has the potential to become sustainable. It is important to observe in figure 4 that the sending agencies, the trellises, are firmly rooted in the soil: the church. They are not independent of the church. However, they also extend into areas outside the church's sphere of influence, becoming an integral part of the support structure with the church but having very different roles and responsibilities. Each current part of this movement must be rooted in the soil of the church, Christ's body, if it is to effectively carry the *missio Dei* forward.

As noted throughout this research journey, understanding who has what role and how they integrate has been unclear and cries out for clarification. Therefore, addressing this need is a valuable and important place to begin. Consequently, to see this integrated model emerge, the strategic plan for growth, outlined in the next section, will focus on partnership relationships within the movement. According to Ivan Liew (2017) in his book *Churches and Mission Agencies Together*, the relationship between the sending church (mission pastor) and the sending agency (agency director) is the key (loc. 1292). When this partnership relationship is delineated and defined, promoting healthy respect and acceptance of each other's role, it will impact their relationships with the missionaries and propel the movement forward. As Liew points out, this relationship "impacts how vision, mission philosophy [policies and procedures] and finances are viewed and practised in the partnership" (loc. 1239).

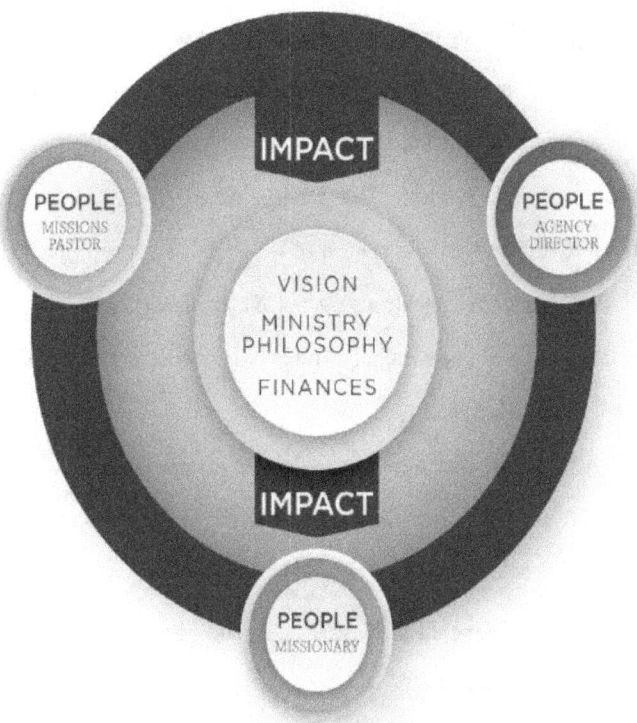

Figure 5: Church-Agency Partnership Model[1]
(Liew 2017, loc. 1290)

---

[1] This diagram is used with permission of the author.

In the following section I intend to outline a strategic plan that will focus on the relationship between the Mongolian churches and mission agencies, hoping that improving understanding and cooperation between both parties will ultimately impact their individual relationships with the cross-cultural missionaries. As mentioned above, when this relationship is on a healthier footing it will bring, God willing, a unity that will impact relationships across the whole movement.

Developing a Strategic Plan for a Stronger Future

This section begins by identifying those involved with the plan and considers their likely response based on the research data before outlining the plan itself. Although there will be a pre-plan meeting to reconnect after two years of restriction and disruption, the plan proper has four elements. This plan is intended to be interactive and informative and will seek to address some of the areas of weaknesses and confusion highlighted in the analysis of chapter 5. It should also be noted that this section is written in the future tense since the plan has not been entirely written or implemented to date due to the above-mentioned reasons.

After the pre-plan meeting, entitled "an inaugural meeting," the following four stages each take one of Ivan Liew's partnership values as the focus of discussion (2017, loc. 912).

1. Establishing the theological and biblical centrality of the church in mission
2. Acknowledging the equal value of church and agency in mission
3. Recognising, respecting and learning to defer to one another's role
4. Discovering how to build one another up and encourage one another

Before outlining the plan in more detail below, the following section introduces the primary people involved and briefly discusses how they might respond to the idea. Please note that I am not excluding the cross-cultural missionaries from the change project but, in the time available, addressing the key relationship in the partnership, which will ultimately impact the missionaries. Meanwhile, the cross-cultural missionaries remain a focal point in the discussion through the work of MMP.

People Involved in the Proposed Strategic Development Plan

The two primary groups of people involved will be the sending agencies and the sending churches. The research showed that each sending church in Mongolia currently has its own particular leadership structure. Only two had a designated leader responsible for the church's missionary activities, including cross-cultural missionaries (CL1; CL7). Conversely, the majority of the sending churches interviewed had a sole lead pastor with, in some cases, a couple of elders or other forms of support leadership structure (CL3; CL4; CL5; CL6). In addition, some of the sending churches are affiliated with denominations and are complicated with an additional level of leadership hierarchy.

This strategic plan will engage participants who cooperated in the research interviews conducted in 2020. I have also established what business consultant John P. Kotter calls a "guiding coalition" (2012, 54). The guiding coalition will be comprised of two key Monoglians within the larger church and missionary community and myself. I have initiated the outline for this plan as someone who has lived among the Mongolians and been involved in the Mongolian church and its missionary ventures for many years. The Mongolians have graciously accepted me as a member of the counsel of MMP and opened the door for this research and its outcomes. In this capacity, I am taking the lead in writing the outline for this plan but then intend to discuss it with both the guiding coalition to ratify it and with the counsel of MMP for implementation. Hopefully, in this manner, I will alleviate any potential uneasiness that could arise from my being a non-Mongolian.

Outlined below are more detailed observations concerning those involved in this project: the church leaders, the sending agency leaders, and those involved in the guiding coalition. Finally, there is the Mongolian Mission Partnership (MMP) through whom this project will be implemented.

Sending Churches Leadership

Seven sending churches participated in the research interviews for this study, representing most of the cross-cultural missionaries who participated in the research. Each of these churches has responsibility for one or more cross-cultural missionary units.[2] These sending church leaders were enthusiastic about being involved in this project, willingly acknowledging the problems highlighted in the research findings and the need to strengthen different aspects of the movement. During the interviews, they were open and frank about the myriad pressures they experience as church leaders in Mongolia. These pressures nearly always centred around the church's general financial requirements which often seem overwhelming and affect its relationship with its cross-cultural missionaries. Focus Group 2, which discussed sustainable finances, noted how money is given for mission but sometimes is necessarily appropriated for other needs deemed more urgent (FG1-3).

Due to such financial pressures most sending church leaders have learnt to commonly equate the term support only with finances rather than considering a broader use of the expression that includes, for example, pastoral care, health and mental wellbeing. This assumption regrettably colours and limits the leaders' view and relationship with their cross-cultural missionaries. For instance, for church leaders in Ulaanbaatar who are unable to meet their own church's immediate financial needs, to

---

[2] A unit is defined as a family or a single person. It has been Pioneers' definition from the beginning and each time consideration is given to making it less impersonal there seems no easier method by which to explain missionary numbers officially.

contemplate sacrificially giving to their cross-cultural missionaries abroad is simply too difficult. Culturally, this inability to give as desired or expected produces a measure of shame in the leaders precipitating a distancing of relationships rather than facing the shame and looking for solutions. This avoidance is made easier because, for all intents and purposes, the missionaries are outside the churches' spheres of awareness for much of the time when on the field.

Sending Agency Leadership

Six missionary sending agencies were involved in this study. The following is a brief breakdown of the six. SA1 is a denomination that has initiated a missions office, although there is currently only one missionary couple under their care (CM6 and CM7). This agency admits it is new, and "leaders of the churches have a poor understanding of it [being a mission office]" (SA1).

SA2 and SA3 represent interCP, a branch of InterCP International under the Korean base. It primarily runs a short-term training facility called Vision School, which introduces young people to mission and then seeks to send them out on a practicum.

Similarly, SA4 is a YWAM sending base and the longest-serving of the four bases in Mongolia. It is responsible for some of the cross-cultural missionaries being sent out. However, they cannot financially support long-term placements with their current system as they rely extensively on financial support from other international organisations or churches. Still, it is worth noting that many of the missionaries interviewed in this research began their journey into mission through the Discipleship Training School (DTS) programme under YWAM.

SA5, Mongolian Missionaries Together (MMT), is one of the few with an official registration and has partnered with Pioneers for about five years. Over recent years SA5 has sent several units onto the mission field but currently has only candidates waiting to go when the pandemic restrictions are lifted. MMT's agency leader single-handedly runs the organisation and was a cross-cultural missionary for many years. She began this agency because of her own missionary experiences and difficulties while on the field, hoping to address some of those difficulties by establishing her own mission agency.

SA6 is an individual instrumental in bringing together what is to be the newly established Mongolian Mission Partnership (MMP). He was previously involved with mission as a church leader, sending cross-cultural missionaries from his church into Asia.

Last, SA7, Diaspora Mongol Network (DMN), operates short-term missions among Mongolians working abroad in neighbouring countries, like Korea and among the Buriat people.[3] Its leader is an elderly gentleman who has Buriat roots and is passionate about the gospel. He often leads these short-term trips.

These six represent a cross-section of the sending capacity in the cross-cultural missionary movement. Each operates independently and each has only a few missionary units under its care. Nevertheless, there is a recognition of the need to work together, but how to do so remains unclear preventing forward momentum.

Mongolian Cross-Cultural Missionary Movement Influencers

Forming a guiding coalition provides a balanced and contextualised approach to this stage of the project. Thus, I asked two experienced Mongolian believers to join the team, both of whom are strategic in their own field of influence. In conversation with each of these strategic individuals it became apparent that we share a concern not just for the relationship between the entities but a desire to see the movement strengthened as a whole.

---

[3] Buriat people are largely focused close to Ulan Ude, Siberia, and in North East China.

The first, Mike[4] (a pseudonym), is in his late forties and was a pastor of one of the largest cell churches in Mongolia during the 1990s. In 2017 God called Mike and his family to serve as cross-cultural missionaries. Through this research, participants identified Mike as a role model within the Mongolian cross-cultural missionary movement. His principal gifting is as a pastor and teacher whose influence and respect are acknowledged within the wider Mongolian church.

The second, Ruth (a pseudonym), is single and in her early forties. For twelve years (2004–2016) she served as director of The Mongolian Mission Center in Erdenet, one of Mongolia's YWAM[5] bases. In 2016, Ruth undertook graduate studies (MA) in America, graduating in 2018. Today Ruth is involved with statistical research for the Mongolian church and is also a valued teacher on mission. I am the third member of this team and the three of us form an informal guiding coalition.

The Mongolian Mission Partnership (MMP)

Since beginning this research one of the exciting things to happen is the official formation of what is called, in English, the Mongolian Mission Partnership (MMP), established with the desire to serve the whole missionary movement and aid in whatever ways it is able to strengthen and build stronger relationships. Its board comprises pastors, teachers, mission leaders and cross-cultural missionaries and two expatriate missionaries (including myself). While still in the forming stage of establishment, MMP encompasses people from across the Mongolian missionary movement, both domestic and cross-cultural, among its members and board.

---

[4] Due to security concerns and for the sake of anonymity I am using pseudonyms for both of these Mongolian co-workers.

[5] Youth With A Mission is a International global missions movement from many cultures seeking to make Jesus known throughout the world. www.ywam.org/about-us/

It is important to mention at this juncture that immediately prior to the decision to embark on this research project, I had an opportunity to be in conversation with some of the key influencers within the Mongolian cross-cultural missionary movement. These conversations sometimes centred around the need for such a body as MMP. I can not claim to have initiated this partnership, only to being a willing catalyst by sowing seeds of encouragement in the formation of what God was already indicating was necessary for the movement to reach the next stage of growth.

The intention of this chapter is to develop a strategy for change and growth that can be enacted by MMP rather than the researcher. Consequently, I intend to present this research, its findings, and its proposals to the MMP counsel, encouraging them to develop it and present it to the wider missionary community as they sense God's leading. Although there might be a risk they may not implement the plan, I believe this is the right route forward because MMP is hungry to see the cross-cultural missionary movement strengthened and sustained. Its heart is to draw all elements of the movement together on the same page, thus building one another up.

How Might the Participants Respond?

The present model of cross-cultural mission including its definition of support appears to have been borrowed from a traditional Western mission model. However, this is a cross-cultural missionary movement emerging from within a Majority-World church. Therefore, the traditional models of cross-cultural mission do not easily fit with what God is doing from the Majority-World. Their structures and organisation stem from a Western mindset rather than a Mongolian or Majority-World basis. It is time to rethink the systems and structures necessary to build a sustainable, contextualised and truly integrated Mongolian cross-cultural missionary movement. Such changes will require adaptive thinking and creativity in order to discover a new way forward to meet the needs of cross-cultural mission from Mongolia. As leadership experts Heifetz and Linsky state,

> Adaptive changes . . . require experiments, new discoveries, and adjustments . . . . Without learning new ways – changing attitudes, values, and behaviors – people cannot make the adaptive leap necessary to thrive in the new environment. (2017, 13)

As a non-Mongolian with no direct form of authority over those involved it is crucial to proceed with care and in all wisdom as one seeking to guide others involved into and through this process. Leadership consultants, Bonem and Patterson, remind us that second chair leaders "begin to have problems when they accidentally cross a line that they failed to recognize. Finding the lines that set your boundaries is a crucial part of the subordinate-leader paradox" (2020, 45).[6] In light of this statement, this project will develop at a pace set by the participants' responses to each stage of the plan rather than by the guiding coalition or MMP, in order to accomplish its goal. I hope in this way to see the line and avoid crossing it.

Existing relationships between the researcher and those involved present a foundation for building and providing a measure of trust paradoxically in an environment of measured distrust. Anthropologist Sherwood Lingenfelter notes that "trust follows when we listen to one another, learn from one another, and then we together frame the work that God has given us to do" (2018, 106). Through the interactive approach of this strategic plan it is hoped that the sending church leaders and agency leaders will be able to listen to each other and together begin to frame what God is teaching them, thus building trust between them.

In summary, this section has identified the key people and relationships to be addressed by this plan. These are the sending church leaders and the sending agencies

---

[6] While Bonem and Patterson originally defined the second chair leader as one with some form of hierarchy within the leadership of an organisation, I am utilising their term here from the sense that, as a non-Monglian, involvement is from the sidelines or only as the voice of counsellor. Therefore, I need to also recognise that invisible line and be careful not to cross it in the process.

who took part in the initial research interview stage. In addition, it acknowledges some of the key influencers within the Mongolian cross-cultural missionary movement, inviting them through the formation of an informal guiding coalition to help shape the final outline of the plan. The concluding piece in this process will be sharing the plan with the Mongolian Mission Partnership and allowing them to implement it. The pace forward is to be deliberate and slow in order to build stronger relationships between these strategic partners in the Mongolian cross-cultural missionary movement, desiring to catalyse a healthy, vibrant relationship between these two groups of people. The following section will consider the strategic plan in more detail.

A Strategy Towards a Stronger Future

As mentioned at the beginning of this section, this is a plan with four elements and four stages, with a pre-plan meeting ahead of the actual plan to reconnect and give an opportunity to outline the proposal to those who will participate. Below each of the stages of this strategic plan is explained in more detail.

Pre-Plan Inaugural Meeting

The initial pre-plan step is to contact and invite the sending church leaders and mission agency leaders to an inaugural meeting. It may not be feasible to assume all of the sending church leaders and or sending agency leaders will be able to attend this meeting. The desire would be for a commitment from at least a quorum of 50 percent of those who participated in the initial interviews. This commitment would allow the possibility of repeating it with the remainder at a later date. This meeting will be informal in nature so that those attending feel comfortable and relaxed, especially at this inaugural meeting as it will set the tone for what is to follow.

Establishing the Centrality of the Church in Mission

This first of the four main stages aims to establish a clearer understanding of the theological bases for mission and recognise the centrality of the church in God's mission. The research has shown an underdeveloped theology of mission within the Mongolian church, contributing to the disunity and consequential breakdown of relationships within the movement. There is no criticism in this finding, only that it reflects the first-generational status of the Mongolian church and that of its emerging cross-cultural missionary movement.

This stage will take the form of an interactive Bible study developed by myself and in relationship with the guiding coalition. I hope to have this study ready sometime during the middle half of 2022. It will focus on the New Testament premiss for mission and God's heart for the church within the *missio Dei*. The goal is to enable the sending church leaders and the sending agency leaders to grasp God's plan and see the church's centrality within that plan of God.

The key ideas are,

1. This is God's mission—the *missio Dei*—Mission is about sending.
2. Jesus was sent into the world to save the world—empowered by the Holy Spirit (Jn 3:16- 17).
3. The church was commissioned by Christ and empowered by the Holy Spirit (Matt 28:19-20; Jn 20:21; Acts 2).
4. God sent Christ into the world. All authority is given to Christ. Christ sends the church to continue the redemptive plan of salvation endowed with authority through the indwelling Holy Spirit.
5. Mission is the responsibility of the church (Rom 10:13-15).

Acknowledging the Equal Value of Church and Agency in Mission

Stage two will focus on the importance and role of the sending agency in the missionary movement. This stage will take as its basis Ralph D. Winter's article in

Perspectives on the World Christian Movement: A Reader (2013) entitled "The Two Structures of God's Redemptive Mission" (244-253). Winter's thesis is that wherever the missionary movement comes from, whether Asia or the West, it will involve two basic structures. He coined the terms "sodalities" and "modalities" for these two structures. For example, Winter considers the New Testament church, structured along Jewish synagogue lines, as a modality. Additionally, there are Paul's missionary bands called and sent out from the Antioch church, who once on the road seem to become self-sufficient yet at other times are dependent on various other churches. These missionary bands are Winter's sodalities. These sodalities consist of those "organized out of committed, experienced workers who affiliated themselves as a second decision beyond membership in the first structure" (Winter 1974, 245). This group is born out of the church, committed to it; yet, in answer to their calling to go, find themselves bound together to a common task beyond their church membership.

While using Winter's article as a basis for this stage, I will also draw on Sam Metcalf's book (2015), *Beyond the Local Church: Now Apostolic Movements Can Change the World,* as a tool for developing this teaching. I hope to have Winter's article translated into Mongolian during the first half of 2022 to make it available to the two members of the guiding coalition. The purpose of this study is to build an interactive discussion aimed at helping clarify the legitimacy of sending agencies and their role within the movement alongside the sending churches, giving an equal weight to the church and agency in mission as two valued expressions of the church.

Recognising, Respecting and Learning to Defer to One Another

Once the first two stages are completed, there should be an appreciation and understanding of the biblical centrality of the church in mission and appreciation of the equal value of sending church and sending agency in mission. Now it is time to turn the attention to the third partnership value. This essentially concerns the responsibilities that these two entities share for the cross-cultural missionaries. Therefore, this stage will first concentrate on who cares for and has oversight of the missionaries. Ivan Liew divides the care of missionaries in this manner; he calls the sending church "the family at home" and the sending agency "the family at work" (2017, loc. 1257).

While the missionary resides in Mongolia the primary care should lay with the sending church. This discussion time will focus on the idea that as the family at home, the sending church must decide how to to support the missionary more fully while in Mongolia. In other words, in what ways might the sending church become the missionary's family at home. Meanwhile, when the missionary returns to the field, the sending agency must decide how to become their family at work and what their responsibilities are in caring for the missionary. These two elements of responsibility have many facets to them. This discussion should not be hurried; rather, it will need a skilful hand to guide the conversation and may take several sessions to agree on these roles and responsibilities. One of the developments of this discussion will be to ask what it looks like to defer to one another in these roles and what it is to submit to one another on an issue. At the time of writing, this stage has yet to be discussed among the guiding coalition for reasons already cited.

Discovering How to Build Up and Encourage One Another

The last of the four partnership values is a time of celebration of the realisation and comprehension of the other three. The idea is simply to come back together after looking through and discussing these partnership values and realise that it is possible to be in fellowship together and find ways to encourage each other in the roles and responsibilities God has given. To consider what has been learnt and how to move forward in growing this missionary movement. Perhaps too, it is good to remember that "trust follows when we listen to one another, learn from one another, and then we together frame the work that God has given us to do" (Lingenfelter 2018, 106).

Timeframe

By the middle of March 2022, the Mongolian government had lifted many of the restrictions that had been in place due to the pandemic, deciding to learn to live with the pandemic rather than fear it. It has been a bold move, and as I write at the end of March 2022, infections are very low. Consequently, I hope to begin regular planning sessions with the guiding coalition during the summer of 2022, aiming to complete the training sessions for the first two stages with a view to beginning this programme after the summer break. Unfortunately, it is difficult to give a more concise timeframe at this stage. Nevertheless, if necessary, I will utilise Zoom or similar platforms to meet with the guiding coalition and more thoroughly plan out this strategy.

Summary

Figure 4 at the beginning of this chapter pictures an integrated cross-cultural missionary movement where the missionaries flourish. Each missionary is planted securely in the soil of the church and firmly supported by the trellis as it extends upwards. However, the research highlighted that this picture does not represent the current movement whose missionaries, on the one hand, are more like separate plants growing out of their church soil (individual pots) but without any strong support structure. On the other hand, others are similar to plants secured to the trellis but without being rooted in the church.

This strategic plan is intended to bring two key parts of this movement together and to discover together God's heart for mission in the New Testament, the centrality of the church in that plan and the equally important supporting role of the sending agency in such a movement. Liew (2017) shows that the four values considered in this model undergird a powerful partnership and will inevitably impact missionary growth. It is a plan with four main stages and an initial meeting to get use to meeting again after COVD restrictions. The four main stages may well encompass many meetings as the participants set the pace and the timeframe to a certain extent. At the same time, it is the desire for the Mongolian Mission Partnership will oversee the implementation of this strategic plan.

Conclusions and Recommendations

This research project began from a place of realising that the cross-cultural missionary movement emerging from within the Mongolian church was simply unsustainable. As the sending churches were unable to serve their missionaries adequately, the missionaries sought the support they needed from either international teams they encountered and joined on the field or from other organisations and churches outside of Mongolia. Some cross-cultural missionaries have been sent out as part of a YWAM team or similar as a practicum of certain training, but again, the YWAM bases have also struggled to financially sustain these short-term missions as they would like.

Despite the challenges, the Mongolian cross-cultural missionary movement remains like a burgeoning infant being fashioned as it grows, not fully able to articulate or meet its needs and so grasping at whatever is at hand. Perhaps the key observation prior to beginning this project is that this movement required a guiding hand and parental-like care through these early years if it is to survive.

Like that infant becoming a toddler there is much curiosity, experimentation and innovation within the movement as it navigates the consequences of growth and recognises the need for some formal structure and boundaries. Out of necessity and in the face of an absence of indigenous structural models, the movement has initially borrowed systems and methods from Western and South Korean missionaries working alongside them in Mongolia. Sadly, these often uncontextualised systems and methods brought unnecessary burdens that, along with the country's socioeconomic situation, inadvertently added increased strain on relationships across the movement. This dissertation has been an attempt to analyse and understand the current movement in order to offer counsel as to a possible way forward for the Mongolians who constitute its sum.

In closing this dissertation, this chapter offers conclusions based on the findings of this research. Second, this chapter will explore the possible implications of these findings for churches beyond Mongolia in other Majority-World nations with a heart for cross-cultural mission, and it will also outline possible personal implications. Third, it will offer recommendations for further studies before concluding with some closing remarks.

Conclusion: Growing and Sustaining a Mongolian Cross-Cultural Missionary Movement

In drawing conclusions from this research, it is good to return to the beginning and reconsider this dissertation's framework. Taking the purpose statement, the goal of the study and the central research issue as outlined in the introduction of this dissertation, this section will consider how these three were met.

First, the purpose of this study was to evaluate the current Mongolian cross-cultural missionary movement and its progress and challenges towards becoming a sustainable indigenous movement now and in the future. It was clear from the literature review of part I that the biggest challenge was the lack of precedent literature concerning the Mongolian church or its first-generation missionary movement. Therefore, through the research process, step one was to assertain what is currently happening within the movement, thus gaining valuable insights in order to evaluate what the next steps might be in moving towards a more indigenous and sustainable future.

In part II, I utilised Howard Brant's *Seven Essentials of Majority World Emerging Mission Movements* (2009) as a framework through which to analyse this missionary movement and ascertain its current strengths and weaknesses. Brant's seven essentials also acted as a launchpad to identifying key elements integral to developing a sustainable cross-cultural missionary movement, which was this dissertation's central research issue (CRI). Brant's seven elements are (i) Called individuals, (ii) Visionary leaders, (iii) Missional churches, (iv) Appropriate training, (v) Flexible structures, (vi) Sustainable finances, and (vii) Powerful prayer movements (2009). From this initial study, four prominant themes emerged creating a fuller picture of what was happening. These themes were: a unity/disunity dichotomy, the influence of their nomadic lifestyle, the need for a more robust theology of mission and the effects of the socioeconomics in Mongolia, and lastly, the influence of the Korean missionary effort to Mongolia. This then led into the goal of this study.

Second, the goal of this study was to draw conclusions based on my findings that can influence the discussion and promote relevant action towards the development of an indigenous group of people who together will facilitate a sustainable Mongolian Cross-cultural missionary movement. From the analysis of the data drawn using Brant's elements as a matrix and from a cultural analysis and utilising two studies undertaken using the work of Hofstede (2010), I was able to draw conclusions concerning the movment's current status and to highlight some of the concerns facing the movement in its challenge to become sustainable. From these insights, I developed a strategic plan designed to foster discussions and promote relevant action towards a more sustainable movement in the future. This plan is to be implemented through the Mongolian Mission Partnership who during the course of this dissertation's time frame have formed as body seeking to serve and encourage the whole movement.

Third, the CRI of this dissertation sought to discover key elements integral to developing a sustainable Mongolian cross-cultural missionary movement within the wider Mongolian Christian context. Throughout this dissertation process, key elements were identified, both within the literature review and through the data analysis process, each element integral to developing and sustaining this movement. Below is a simple diagram incorporating all the discoveries of this dissertation. Central are the three bodies that currently make up the movement showing how their spheres of influence intersect, highlighting the key relationships while being surrounded by the core elements necessary for a flourishing Mongolian cross-cultural missionary movement. Above are the four partnership elements of the strategic plan for strengthening key relationships.

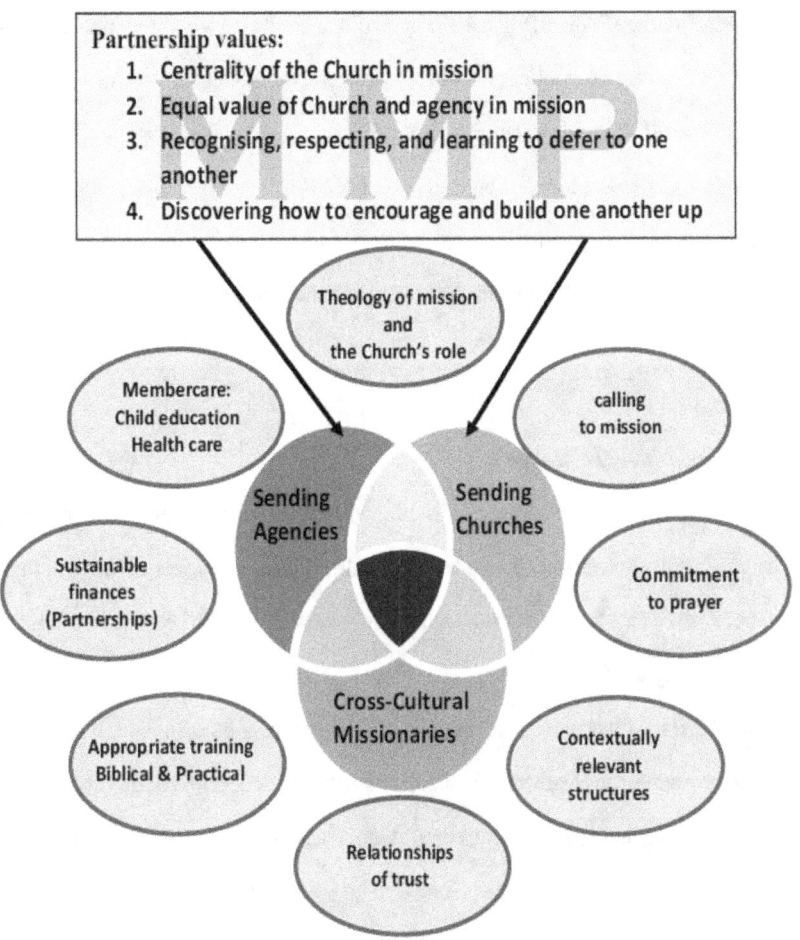

Figure 6: Pictorial Summary of the Dissertation Discoveries.

Finally, perhaps the most significant influence upon all of these findings and the proposed strategic plan is the formation of the MMP which emerged during the time frame of this research project. This umbrella organisation consisting of individuals from those involved with the missionary movement has the potential to serve and encourage this movement through its growth stage and beyond. Before MMP was formed various and often conflicting influences offered services to the movement at different points along the journey. Now MMP has the potential to be the vehicle through which those other services are channelled and sifted. Therefore, the strategic plan will be most effective if MMP is able to embrace it, teach it and develop it because, while there are two missionaries to Mongolia on the counsel of MMP, myself included, it has a Mongolian head. This will place the outcome of this research project squarely and rightly into the hands of the Mongolians as a catalyst in the process of growing a sustainable movement.

Implications Beyond Mongolia

While this study is specifically Mongolian in focus it does not preclude it from having implications within the wider cross-cultural missionary world. Many of the nations in which Mongolian cross-cultural missionaries seek to serve have a similar recent history to Mongolia. Many were former satellite states of the former USSR in Central Asia, with equally small populations. The scares of the Soviet influence are common and lessons learned in Mongolia and strategies developed to overcome these influences may help these other Central Asian countries. The outworking of this research's strategic plan has the potential to be used in these other countries. Currently, these countries are open and even seek Mongolian influence due to their common historical bonds.

The Mongolian cross-cultural missionary movement can also become a valuable case study for other Majority-World nations as missionary movements emerge. Of course, it is a work in progress, much like the early church and Paul's missionary bands. Yet time and again, the book of Acts and Paul's letters provide infinite wisdom into establishing the work of the church. So too, I trust emerging movements like this one will help provide insight into the work of God and God's church in this new age of post-Christendom.

Finally, for long-term missionary to Mongolia, this study is significant in understanding the complexities of an emerging Majority-World cross-cultural missionary movement. To be effective in giving counsel it is important that I am aware of what God is doing among this new Mongolian generation. As I prepare to consider leaving Mongolia after thirty years, I want to leave them with a study that will challenge, encourage and catalyse the movement forward.

Recommendations for Further Studies

During the research phase of this study, several areas that could become research projects in themselves became apparent. The first is to research the correlation between economic standing and successful cross-cultural missionary growth in a national church. This research considered two examples, the missionary movement from South Korea and Singapore, both of which developed strong economies during which time the church developed strong missionary movements. This fact would suggest that further study into this correlation and what it might mean for poorer or more fragile economies and its consequential effect on cross-cultural missionary activity would be an area to study.

Second, as highlighted in the literature review, a study into what constitutes a truly contextualised Mongolian church is essential. It was missionaries to Mongolia in the early 1990s who established the church in Mongolia. At that time, most of the missionaries' cultural awareness was limited; therefore, what was established was what was known by the missionary. From these humble beginnings, the church in Mongolia began a tradition as a first-generation church. Yet, what actually constitutes a Mongolian church? This question significantly impacts the missionary movement out of such a church.

Third, the two focus groups' ongoing discussions surrounding the possibilities of raising capital support for cross-cultural mission and the need to establish educational opportunities for children of cross-cultural missionaries are both areas of further research for the Mongolian church to undertake. Concerning sustainable finances, it was acknowledged during the focus group discussions that churches prioritise their giving but giving to mission is not necessarily the highest priority, meaning it often gets redirected. Even with a commitment to mission giving there is simply not enough to cover the needs of this growing movement. Therefore, creative opportunities need to be explored further. Children's education also requires further study into what is available and amenable for the Mongolian cross-cultural missionary movement so that Mongolian missionary families can sustain the education of their children while serving cross-culturally.

Concluding Remarks

This study aimed to evaluate the current Mongolian cross-cultural missionary movement and its progress towards becoming a sustainable movement. I believe that this outcome has been in part achieved or initiated by this study.

Finally, I hope this research study will be instrumental in drawing the church, the Mongolian missionaries, and the sending churches closer together in working towards a productive partnership where all are rooted in the church but recognise clear roles and responsibilities. In turn, this integration should draw all three entities closer towards the unity found at the heart of the movement (see figure 6), where all parts intersect and merge into one unified oal: the fulfilment of the *missio Dei*.

www.ingramcontent.com/pod-product-compliance
Lightning Source LLC
Chambersburg PA
CBHW071453080526
44587CB00014B/2095